Joyce Appleby on *Thomas Jefferson*
Louis Auchincloss on *Theodore Roosevelt*
Jean H. Baker on *James Buchanan*
H. W. Brands on *Woodrow Wilson*
Alan Brinkley on *John F. Kennedy*
Douglas Brinkley on *Gerald R. Ford*
Josiah Bunting III on *Ulysses S. Grant*
James MacGregor Burns and Susan Dunn on *George Washington*
Charles W. Calhoun on *Benjamin Harrison*
Gail Collins on *William Henry Harrison*
Robert Dallek on *Harry S. Truman*
John W. Dean on *Warren G. Harding*
John Patrick Diggins on *John Adams*
Elizabeth Drew on *Richard M. Nixon*
John S. D. Eisenhower on *Zachary Taylor*
Paul Finkelman on *Millard Fillmore*
Annette Gordon-Reed on *Andrew Johnson*
Henry F. Graff on *Grover Cleveland*
David Greenberg on *Calvin Coolidge*
Gary Hart on *James Monroe*
Michael F. Holt on *Franklin Pierce*
Roy Jenkins on *Franklin Delano Roosevelt*
Zachary Karabell on *Chester Alan Arthur*
William E. Leuchtenburg on *Herbert Hoover*
James Mann on *George W. Bush*
Gary May on *John Tyler*
George McGovern on *Abraham Lincoln*
Timothy Naftali on *George H. W. Bush*
Charles Peters on *Lyndon B. Johnson*
Kevin Phillips on *William McKinley*
Robert V. Remini on *John Quincy Adams*
Jeffrey Rosen on *William Howard Taft*
Ira Rutkow on *James A. Garfield*
John Seigenthaler on *James K. Polk*
Hans L. Trefousse on *Rutherford B. Hayes*
Jacob Weisberg on *Ronald Reagan*
Tom Wicker on *Dwight D. Eisenhower*
Ted Widmer on *Martin Van Buren*
Sean Wilentz on *Andrew Jackson*
Garry Wills on *James Madison*
Julian E. Zelizer on *Jimmy Carter*

George W. Bush

James Mann

George W. Bush

THE AMERICAN PRESIDENTS

ARTHUR M. SCHLESINGER, JR., AND SEAN WILENTZ

GENERAL EDITORS

Times Books

HENRY HOLT AND COMPANY, NEW YORK

Times Books
Henry Holt and Company, LLC
Publishers since 1866
175 Fifth Avenue
New York, New York 10010
www.henryholt.com

Frontispiece: © Pool/Getty Images

Library of Congress Cataloging-in-Publication Data
Mann, Jim, 1946–
George W. Bush / James Mann.—First edition.
    pages cm.—(The American presidents series)
Includes bibliographical references and index.
ISBN 978-0-8050-9397-1 (hardcover)—ISBN 978-1-62779-230-1
(electronic book) 1. Presidents—United States—Biography. 2. United
States—Politics and government—2001–2009. I. Title.
E902.M344 2015
973.931092—dc23
[B]
                                                          2014026687

First Edition 2015

Printed in the United States of America
1 3 5 7 9 10 8 6 4 2

To Nate, Ben, and Ryan

Contents

Editor's Note

THE AMERICAN PRESIDENCY

The president is the central player in the American political order. That would seem to contradict the intentions of the Founding Fathers. Remembering the horrid example of the British monarchy, they invented a separation of powers in order, as Justice Brandeis later put it, "to preclude the exercise of arbitrary power." Accordingly, they divided the government into three allegedly equal and coordinate branches—the executive, the legislative, and the judiciary.

But a system based on the tripartite separation of powers has an inherent tendency toward inertia and stalemate. One of the three branches must take the initiative if the system is to move. The executive branch alone is structurally capable of taking that initiative. The Founders must have sensed this when they accepted Alexander Hamilton's proposition in the Seventieth Federalist that "energy in the executive is a leading character in the definition of good government." They thus envisaged a strong president—but within an equally strong system of constitutional accountability. (The term *imperial presidency* arose in the 1970s to describe the situation when the balance between power and accountability is upset in favor of the executive.)

The American system of self-government thus comes to focus in the presidency—"the vital place of action in the system," as

Woodrow Wilson put it. Henry Adams, himself the great-grandson and grandson of presidents as well as the most brilliant of American historians, said that the American president "resembles the commander of a ship at sea. He must have a helm to grasp, a course to steer, a port to seek." The men in the White House (thus far only men, alas) in steering their chosen courses have shaped our destiny as a nation.

Biography offers an easy education in American history, rendering the past more human, more vivid, more intimate, more accessible, more connected to ourselves. Biography reminds us that presidents are not supermen. They are human beings too, worrying about decisions, attending to wives and children, juggling balls in the air, and putting on their pants one leg at a time. Indeed, as Emerson contended, "There is properly no history; only biography."

Presidents serve us as inspirations, and they also serve us as warnings. They provide bad examples as well as good. The nation, the Supreme Court has said, has "no right to expect that it will always have wise and humane rulers, sincerely attached to the principles of the Constitution. Wicked men, ambitious of power, with hatred of liberty and contempt of law, may fill the place once occupied by Washington and Lincoln."

The men in the White House express the ideals and the values, the frailties and the flaws, of the voters who send them there. It is altogether natural that we should want to know more about the virtues and the vices of the fellows we have elected to govern us. As we know more about them, we will know more about ourselves. The French political philosopher Joseph de Maistre said, "Every nation has the government it deserves."

At the start of the twenty-first century, forty-two men have made it to the Oval Office. (George W. Bush is counted our forty-third president, because Grover Cleveland, who served nonconsecutive terms, is counted twice.) Of the parade of presidents, a dozen or so lead the polls periodically conducted by historians and political scientists. What makes a great president?

Great presidents possess, or are possessed by, a vision of an ideal America. Their passion, as they grasp the helm, is to set the ship of state on the right course toward the port they seek. Great presidents also have a deep psychic connection with the needs, anxieties, dreams of people. "I do not believe," said Wilson, "that any man can lead who does not act . . . under the impulse of a profound sympathy with those whom he leads—a sympathy which is insight—an insight which is of the heart rather than of the intellect."

"All of our great presidents," said Franklin D. Roosevelt, "were leaders of thought at a time when certain ideas in the life of the nation had to be clarified." So Washington incarnated the idea of federal union, Jefferson and Jackson the idea of democracy, Lincoln union and freedom, Cleveland rugged honesty. Theodore Roosevelt and Wilson, said FDR, were both "moral leaders, each in his own way and his own time, who used the presidency as a pulpit."

To succeed, presidents not only must have a port to seek but they must convince Congress and the electorate that it is a port worth seeking. Politics in a democracy is ultimately an educational process, an adventure in persuasion and consent. Every president stands in Theodore Roosevelt's bully pulpit.

The greatest presidents in the scholars' rankings, Washington, Lincoln, and Franklin Roosevelt, were leaders who confronted and overcame the republic's greatest crises. Crisis widens presidential opportunities for bold and imaginative action. But it does not guarantee presidential greatness. The crisis of secession did not spur Buchanan or the crisis of depression spur Hoover to creative leadership. Their inadequacies in the face of crisis allowed Lincoln and the second Roosevelt to show the difference individuals make to history. Still, even in the absence of first-order crisis, forceful and persuasive presidents—Jefferson, Jackson, James K. Polk, Theodore Roosevelt, Harry Truman, John F. Kennedy, Ronald Reagan, George W. Bush—are able to impose their own priorities on the country.

The diverse drama of the presidency offers a fascinating set of tales. Biographies of American presidents constitute a chronicle of wisdom and folly, nobility and pettiness, courage and cunning, forthrightness and deceit, quarrel and consensus. The turmoil perennially swirling around the White House illuminates the heart of the American democracy.

It is the aim of the American Presidents series to present the grand panorama of our chief executives in volumes compact enough for the busy reader, lucid enough for the student, authoritative enough for the scholar. Each volume offers a distillation of character and career. I hope that these lives will give readers some understanding of the pitfalls and potentialities of the presidency and also of the responsibilities of citizenship. Truman's famous sign—"The buck stops here"—tells only half the story. Citizens cannot escape the ultimate responsibility. It is in the voting booth, not on the presidential desk, that the buck finally stops.

—Arthur M. Schlesinger, Jr.

George W. Bush

Prologue

During the 2000 presidential campaign, it was frequently said of George W. Bush that he had almost never set foot outside the United States. News articles repeatedly specified that, other than Mexico, he had made only three trips outside the United States in his life: one to China; one to Rome, Israel, and Egypt; and one to Gambia to represent his father's administration. Commentators often rehashed this reporting, taking this skimpy list as evidence of his seeming provinciality and lack of curiosity.

Thus, I was quite startled when, in writing a previous book about George W. Bush's foreign-policy team, I ran across a casual remark Bush made in 2003 on the eve of a presidential trip to Britain. The interviewer David Frost asked if this was Bush's first visit to London. "I've been there a couple of times," Bush answered. "I remember Laura and I went to see 'Cats' in London. Gosh, I remember going to some nice pubs in London." Some further checking turned up the information that Bush had, in fact, made several trips to Europe in the 1980s and 1990s, stopping in London, Scotland, Paris, Spain, and Portugal, among other places, mostly as part of a business group, the Young Presidents' Organization. He and his advisers did not bother to correct the news stories in the 2000 campaign; if the impression formed that he was unsophisticated, that was of little concern (and could even help with some voters).

That episode provides a fitting introduction to the life of George W. Bush. With Bush, appearances were frequently deceiving. He styled himself as a common man and tough-talking Texan, yet he came from a world of wealth, private schooling, and privilege. He was among the most unpopular of U.S. presidents, reviled by millions of Americans, yet those who met him in person usually found him to be likable and charming. He was caricatured as stupid, an impression furthered by his many malapropisms, yet those who worked with or for him often reported him to be surprisingly canny. Politically, too, impressions of Bush were often misleading: he held himself out as a strong conservative yet, in the end, he angered the political right with big-government programs such as Medicare prescription drug benefits and the TARP program during the financial crisis.

He was only the second president in American history whose father had previously held the job, following the path of John Quincy Adams in the early nineteenth century. His relationship with his father, George H. W. Bush, had often been a preoccupying factor in his life. When he was a boy, he was sometimes known as Little George. When he first became involved in politics, helping out in his father's political campaigns, he was called Junior, a name he disliked. Eventually, the nickname that stuck for years was the middle initial that distinguished him from his father: he was "W" (or, in Texas, "Dub-ya").

Once, while his father was vice president, he heard someone speak casually about the difficulties of being a "PK," a preacher's kid. "You think that's tough?" asked Bush, who was then nearly forty years old. "Try being a VPK [a vice president's kid]." Soon after his father became president, George W. Bush ordered a campaign adviser to prepare a written report for him on what happened to the children of American presidents. The survey found that while a few went on to successful careers, many others were ne'er-do-wells, damaged by the burden of their powerful, successful fathers.

The fact that he was a president's son hovered in the background throughout George W. Bush's presidency. It sometimes colored how his policies were perceived and portrayed. When he first came to the White House, his presidency was said to be a "retread" of his father's administration. Later on, after he carried out policies very different from those of his father, the commentary changed: it was said that he must somehow harbor some sort of oedipal resentment.

Bush himself showed signs of sensitivity on this subject. "The one somewhat touchy area between us—never openly discussed—was my close relationship to the president's father," wrote Robert M. Gates, Bush's second defense secretary, who had previously held senior positions in the George H. W. Bush administration. When Gates was first approached about the Pentagon job in late 2006 and was asked to talk with the president, he first consulted quietly with Bush's father. Soon he proceeded to an interview with George W. Bush, who told Gates, wrongly, that his father didn't know the job offer was in the works.

Nevertheless, George H. W. Bush turned out to be largely irrelevant to George W. Bush's presidency. The younger Bush confronted a series of problems his father never faced, ranging from the September 11 attacks to Hurricane Katrina to the global financial crisis. And by the time the president left office, his father was an afterthought. George W. Bush became undeniably his own man, launching initiatives and making mistakes that were all his own, arousing passions both positive and negative of the sort that his father never attracted.

• • •

George W. Bush was president at a critical juncture in American history. The attacks of September 11 marked the only time since Pearl Harbor or the War of 1812 that there was a direct foreign attack on American soil. That day brought to an end the sense of calm, security, and triumphalism that had prevailed in the United States following the end of the cold war.

America had entered the new millennium at the peak of its power. At home, the U.S. economy had grown rapidly through the 1990s; one of the reigning economic questions at the time Bush took office was what to do about the large surpluses the federal budget was running. On the world stage, America faced no serious rival as a global power.

Eight years later, at the end of Bush's term, the United States was struggling to regain its stature abroad and its prosperity at home. The actions Bush took were often (though not always) a contributing factor in the country's reversal of fortune. The question of what might have happened if someone else were president is the sort of counterfactual that can be debated endlessly. There can be no doubt, however, that Bush's presidency marked a troubled entry into the twenty-first century for the United States and a turning point in its self-confident approach to the world. It was, by any standard, one of the most consequential presidencies in American history.

1

"A Good-Time Guy"

The family of George W. Bush had prospered since the nineteenth century on its close connections, first to American manufacturing and finance and then, eventually, to politics. George W. Bush's great-grandfather Samuel Bush was a railroad and steel executive. His grandfather Prescott Bush was a prominent Wall Street investment banker who was later elected to the U.S. Senate from Connecticut in 1952. His father, George H. W. Bush, became an oil executive in his early adult years, prior to entering politics, at first unsuccessfully, before finally rising to be president of the United States.

At the time George W. Bush was born, his father, then twenty-two years old, was still an undergraduate at Yale University, completing his college education after service in World War II. His twenty-one-year-old mother, a former debutante named Barbara Pierce, had had a difficult pregnancy, having gained more than sixty pounds, and was unable to deliver until, on her mother-in-law's advice, she finally took some castor oil. It worked. George W. Bush was born on July 6, 1946, in New Haven, Connecticut, a town that would years later come to symbolize his lifetime resentment of East Coast elites and intellectuals.

The baby was nicknamed Georgie. He became, in his mother's words, "a much beloved and slightly spoiled little boy." When he was two, his parents moved to West Texas as his father forsook Wall Street to pursue a career in the oil business. He was offered a job as a trainee in Texas by one of his own father's business partners.

The Bushes moved first to Odessa, Texas, and then settled in 1950 in the town of Midland, a hot, dusty city that lay over the mammoth oil and gas fields of the Permian Basin. They spent the entire decade of the 1950s in Midland, participating fully in its weekly rituals: Friday nights at the high school football games, Sunday mornings at church, Mondays on foot to the local public school.

For his parents, raised in privileged enclaves in Greenwich, Connecticut, and Rye, New York, relocation to Texas was simply a career move and stepping-stone. By contrast, for George W. Bush, who spent his entire childhood there, Midland carried far deeper significance, lodging itself at the core of his personality, his worldview, his cultural outlook, and, eventually, his political identity. The younger Bush portrayed himself to the public as someone distant from the sophisticated lands of the East and West Coasts. In his own self-image, growing up in Midland was what distinguished him from his father. Even as George W. attended private schools and elite Eastern universities and benefited from his family's name and connections, he always emphasized his West Texas roots. As a rising politician, when he was asked how he was different from his father, he would often reply: "I went to Sam Houston Elementary School in Midland, Texas, and he went to Greenwich Country Day School in Connecticut." On occasion, he even portrayed Texas's biggest cities as outside his realm. In 1995, on his first day as governor, Bush told a Texas state legislator, "Just remember, I'm from Midland, not Dallas." He became skilled, indeed shrewd, at assuming the role of the small-town Texas country boy.

The event that shaped Bush's childhood was the death of his sister Robin. Three years younger than George W., she was diagnosed with leukemia in early 1953, not long after the birth of the Bushes' third child, Jeb. The Bush parents hurriedly brought Robin to New York City for advanced care and proceeded to shuttle back and forth regularly for her tests and treatment, leaving seven-year-old George W. in Midland with friends. He was spared the details on how sick Robin was. "We thought he was too young to know," Barbara Bush later explained. After seven months, Robin died in New York. The Bushes flew home, drove to their son's elementary school, brought him out to the car, and told him the news. He was stunned, asking his mother several times, "Why didn't you tell me?"

In the months that followed, George W. seemed to take on the job of consoling his parents, particularly his mother. George H. W. Bush, rising in the oil business, was working long hours and was often on the road. Barbara Bush, whose hair turned white during Robin's illness, was home alone with George W. and the infant Jeb. "I must say, George Junior saved my life," she told an interviewer years later. Once, when one of George W.'s friends asked him to play outside, he said he had to stay home to take care of his mother. Years later, Bush reflected that his mother's response to Robin's death had been "to envelop herself completely around me. She kind of smothered me and then recognized it was the wrong thing to do."

The result was that George W. looked up to his father as a model, yet was closer to his mother and identified with her. "I picked up a lot of Mother's personality," he wrote in his memoir. He and his mother had similar senses of humor, similar habits of teasing and needling; they took similar delight in being blunt and irreverent. Later in life, George W. would joke to audiences that he possessed his father's eyes but his mother's mouth.

His father was by nature driven, high-achieving, respectful and respectable, controlled, prudent, loyal, polite, and dutiful. As a teenager and young man, George W. had the opposite traits. He was less driven than his father, less serious in his approach to life, and far less eager to convey an air of gravitas. Instead, he was cocky, mischievous, fun-loving, garrulous, and hotheaded—a curious blend of charm and cynicism. He admired his father but was disdainful of the established, East Coast–oriented world from which his father arose.

In 1959, as George H. W. Bush's oil ventures began to shift from inland Texas to offshore drilling, the family moved to Houston. George W. attended a local private school, Kinkaid, for two years and was then sent off to the Northeast to get a traditional Bush family education. His parents enrolled him at Phillips Academy in Andover, Massachusetts, one of the country's leading prep schools, where his father had stood out as class president and captain of the baseball and soccer teams. George W. was given no choice; his father brought him to Andover for a tour, and, months later, his mother told him he had been accepted and would go there. His friends in Texas thought he was somehow being punished and sent away to boarding school for doing something wrong.

For George W., the school was at first terrifying. "Going to Andover was the hardest thing I did in my life, until I ran for president," he later wrote. One of his early assignments in English class was to describe a significant emotional experience; Bush, not surprisingly, chose to write about Robin's death. After using the word "tears" once in his essay, he looked for a synonym so as to avoid repetition. Pulling out the thesaurus that Barbara Bush had packed for him, he put it to use: "The lacerates ran down my cheek," he wrote. It was an early sign of the weakness for malapropisms for which he would become famous. The teacher not only gave him a failing grade on the essay but told Bush his writing was terrible. He reacted by calling home and saying he was unhappy at Andover. His parents persuaded him to stay.

Gradually, he decided to play a different role at Andover from that of his father. George H. W. Bush had excelled at athletics and formal activities like Student Council. By the account of Clay Johnson, George W.'s lifetime friend, fellow Texan, and Andover classmate, the younger Bush determined that his own mission would be "to instill a sense of frivolity" at the school.

His own gift lay in his social skills. He made friends easily. He gradually emerged at the center of an in-crowd, one that walked around the school with "a little swagger." It was also at Andover that those around him first remarked on his distinctive smirk, the smile, mouth turned down, that reflected bemusement or sarcasm or self-deprecation.

He became Andover's lead cheerleader. At one point, he was photographed in a skit posing as a girl in a sweater to ridicule a rival team. In his senior year, he was known above all for organizing a stickball league with elaborate rules; it even issued its own registration cards, sometimes with phony ages that could be used for fake IDs. In a poll of his Andover classmates, Bush came in second in the category of "big man on campus."

His grades were not outstanding. His college board scores (566 in verbal skills, 640 in math) were similarly unimpressive. When George W. told Andover's dean that he wanted to go to Yale, the dean advised him to be sure to apply as well to some colleges where he would be more likely to gain admission. George W. took a tour with his father of the University of Texas in Austin and began to envision himself as a student there. But the cautious Andover dean had overestimated the degree to which Yale had become a meritocracy. In 1964, when George W. was applying to the college, his grandfather had recently stepped down after two terms as a U.S. senator from Connecticut, Yale's home state, and his father was preparing to run for the U.S. Senate in Texas. Besides his father, grandfather, and great-great-grandfather, so many uncles and cousins from both sides of his family had gone to Yale that, when one written form asked applicants if any relatives had gone to the school, George W.'s list was so long he had to write on the back of the page. There was simply no way that Yale was going to refuse to admit George W. Bush, even if his academic credentials were less than outstanding.

After Andover, Yale was easy. George W. had already made the transition from living at home. He roomed with two of his prep school friends, along with a fourth student whose father had also gone to Yale. He majored in history but didn't take academics particularly seriously; for a class on oratory, he drafted a speech nominating Red Sox star Carl Yastrzemski to be mayor of Boston.

He became known above all as "a good-time guy," as his college friend the football star Calvin Hill later put it. He eventually became a member of Skull and Bones, the exclusive Yale secret society to which his father and grandfather had both been admitted. But that was merely a senior-year activity; for most of George W.'s college career his campus life centered on Delta Kappa Epsilon (DKE), one of Yale's (nonresident) fraternities. DKE was known on campus as the fraternity for athletes and a haven for drinking and parties; Bush became its president, its top prankster and instigator, the organizer of its first toga party.

The first time George W. Bush's name ever appeared in the *New York Times*, it was to defend his fraternity. In 1967, amid the turmoil of antiwar protests sweeping college campuses, the *Yale Daily News* reported that DKE had "branded" forty of its new recruits by applying a hot coat hanger to their backs in a way that singed into the flesh the Greek letter delta. Bush minimized the significance of the episode, telling the *Times* that the branding caused "only a cigarette burn."

Campus pranks led to a couple of minor run-ins with the police. Once, Bush and his friends seized a Christmas wreath from a local hotel to decorate the DKE house for a party; they were charged with disorderly conduct, but the charges were dropped. Years later, after he entered politics, Bush developed a clever tautology to deflect questions about these and other episodes from his college days and early adulthood. "When I was young and irresponsible," he said, "I was young and irresponsible."

But there were a few aspects to life at Yale that left Bush unhappy and embittered, then and for decades afterward. They centered on intellectuals, national politics, and the views expressed on campus about his father. In the fall of George W.'s freshman year, his father ran for the U.S. Senate in Texas against the incumbent Democrat, Ralph Yarborough. It was one of the most prominent Senate races that year, covered on the front pages of national newspapers and the *Yale Daily News*, so that most students knew who George H. W. Bush was and could identify George W. as his son.

Although Bush's father would later become known as a moderate Republican, in that 1964 campaign he ran as a hard conservative and was a strong supporter of the Republican presidential nominee Barry Goldwater. (He gave Goldwater's book *The Conscience of a Conservative* to George W. with instructions to read it.) In that campaign, George H. W. Bush also took a strong position against the historic legislation that became the 1964 Civil Rights Act, opposed the nuclear test ban treaty, and called for U.S. withdrawal from the United Nations if Communist China were admitted.

George W. went home to Texas to help his father in the final days of the campaign. His father lost, and the result was a profound disappointment to the entire family. Upon his return to Yale, however, George W. found that many of his fellow students were happy with the election results. In one encounter he remembered for decades, Bush ran into the college's famed chaplain William Sloane Coffin Jr., an Andover and Yale classmate of his father. Coffin had been actively involved in the Freedom Rides and sit-ins of the civil rights movement. Appalled by George H. W. Bush's opposition to civil rights legislation, Coffin told George W. that his father had lost to "a better man." The younger Bush was infuriated.

It was one of many such slights Bush perceived at Yale, both to his father and to the traditional, fraternity-centered life he was leading. Yale was not a meritocracy; Bush's very presence on campus was testimony to that fact. But the college was becoming more so than it had ever been in the past, and as a result the climate at Yale was shifting. Amid the upsurge in student activism of the 1960s, quite a few students looked down upon the drinking, party-loving culture of Bush and his friends. Bush's father went on to win a congressional seat from Houston in 1966 and became a supporter of the war in Vietnam; so, therefore, did his son. But the younger Bush was not so much politically conservative at college as he was apolitical.

Bush told an interviewer a quarter century later that he had been irritated by the "snobs" at Yale. "What angered me was the way such people at Yale felt so intellectually superior and so righteous," he said. He harbored a grudge against Yale for decades and did not attend college reunions. This disdain was his own, not a sentiment shared by his friends. At the time of Bush's twenty-fifth reunion in 1993, his old roommate Clay Johnson was fund-raising for the college and called to ask Bush how much he wanted to give. "I want to give nothing," Bush told him.

Only after Bush became president did he seek to make amends. In May 2003, only two months after the invasion of Iraq, Bush opened the White House to his Yale classmates for a night in honor of their thirty-fifth reunion. Despite the passions over the war, the event went surprisingly smoothly. Some of those who had looked down on Bush at Yale came away surprised by how adept he was in a social setting. One of Bush's classmates was Leilani Akwai, a transsexual whose name at Yale had been Peter Akwai. Approaching the president in the White House receiving line, she introduced herself and said, "I guess the last time we spoke, I was still living as a man." Bush replied graciously, "But now you're you."

Bush graduated in 1968, just as the Vietnam War was reaching its peak. That year, American troop deployments surpassed 500,000, and more than 16,000 Americans were killed. Speaking at Bush's graduation, Yale president Kingman Brewster criticized the military draft, asserting that it forced students into "a cynical, evasive gamesmanship" to avoid military service. Some of Bush's classmates became conscientious objectors, went to Canada, or obtained medical deferments to keep from being sent to Vietnam.

Bush pursued a different plan. During his Christmas vacation in 1967, he began to ask about joining the Texas Air National Guard's 147th Fighter Group and learned there might be some openings for pilots. He took a pilot's aptitude test that spring, received a low but passing grade, and formally enlisted in the unit in Houston in late May, less than two weeks before his graduation from Yale made him eligible for the draft.

The National Guard unit Bush joined was responsible for defending Texas and neighboring states from the unlikely possibility that the United States could be attacked from the South, through Mexico or the Caribbean. Members of the 147th Fighter Group were not assigned to Vietnam unless they volunteered. During this era, the Texas National Guard became known as a "champagne" unit. Along with Bush, its ranks included the sons of three of the state's other leading political figures, Governor John Connally, Senator John Tower, and Representative Lloyd Bentsen, along with at least seven members of the Dallas Cowboys.

Bush obtained a slot in this Guard unit with help both from his father's friends and from another of Texas's most powerful political figures, Ben Barnes, the speaker of the Texas legislature. Bush would later assert that neither his father, then a congressman, nor any other member of the Bush family ever directly contacted anyone in the Guard. This statement appears to be true. However, a Houston oil executive named Sidney Adger, who was a friend of Bush's father, contacted Barnes, who in turn got in touch with National Guard officials to urge that George W. be given one of the slots for a pilot. Guard officials had plenty of reasons to accommodate a congressman's son. One Guard leader, Colonel Walter "Buck" Staudt, who was active in helping George W. land a position in the Guard, traveled to Washington a few months later to lobby Congressman Bush for more money for Houston's Ellington Air Force Base.

In the fall of 1968, after completing basic training, George W. was given time off to go to Florida and work in the Senate campaign of the Republican candidate Edward Gurney before continuing on to flight school. It was merely one of several occasions when Bush was accorded treatment that went beyond that of an ordinary guardsman. On one occasion, while Bush was in flight training in Valdosta, Georgia, President Richard Nixon dispatched a plane to bring George W. to Washington for an introductory date with his daughter Tricia. (There was no second date.) When George W. graduated from flight school, George H. W. Bush gave the commencement address and pinned first lieutenant wings on his son.

• • •

In 1970, once his two years of active duty were completed, George W. settled in Houston, where he continued his Guard obligations by flying F-102 jets at Ellington Air Force Base. That year, his father ran for the Senate again against the Democratic candidate Lloyd Bentsen. George W. helped out when he could, occasionally appearing on the campaign plane in his flight jacket. But his father lost again. Soon afterward, Nixon appointed George H. W. Bush to be the U.S. ambassador to the United Nations, and he and Barbara moved to New York City.

George W. remained in Houston. He lived in a singles complex and worked at a local agribusiness run by one of his father's associates. The job was boring; he would later recall that at one point he found himself conducting a study of the mushroom industry. In the spring of 1972, Jimmy Allison, a family friend who had run George H. W. Bush's successful campaign for Congress, recruited George W. to work as the political director for the Senate campaign of former Postmaster General Winton Blount in Alabama. Texas National Guard officials permitted Bush to move to Montgomery, with the stipulation that he should continue his Guard duty there. But while he worked on the Blount campaign, his attendance with the Alabama National Guard was infrequent at best. He did not resume his duty with the Texas National Guard for a year. A few months after his return, he was granted an expedited release from his Guard obligations so that he could go to business school.

His father had been a pilot, shot down over the Pacific in World War II. George W. Bush was a pilot, too, but his stint in the National Guard became a political liability, an issue that would become the subject of repeated investigations, first in his father's presidential campaign in 1988 and then in George W.'s own campaigns for governor of Texas and the presidency.

The accusations of favoritism always lingered. Bush was clearly given greater leeway than an ordinary Guard member, though perhaps no more than the sons of other prominent political figures like Bentsen and Connally.

• • •

In December 1972, George W. Bush, then twenty-six years old and nearing the end of his National Guard duty, gathered with his family in Washington for the Christmas holidays. His parents had just moved there from New York City so that George H. W. Bush could start a new job as chairman of the Republican National Committee.

One night, George W. brought his fifteen-year-old brother Marvin with him to a party, where both of them were drinking. On the way back, George W.'s car hit a neighbor's trash can and carried it down the block. Once they were home, his father sent word that he wanted George W. to come see him in the den. George W. was in no mood for a polite lecture. "I hear you're looking for me," he told his father. "You wanna go mano a mano right here?" The confrontation ended without a fight when George W.'s brother Jeb interceded to calm him down.

It was a raw, tense confrontation. In his memoir four decades later, George W. reflected, "I was a boozy kid, and he was an understandably irritated father." Those words were a fitting summation of his life in the early 1970s. George W. Bush was drifting. He dabbled in politics, thought of going back to school, moved from Texas to Alabama and back, tried one job and then another. Throughout the period, his self-description as a "boozy kid" remained apt.

Bush would later describe the aimlessness of these early-adult years as a matter of choice. He said he viewed the decade after college as a time to explore, explaining that he did not want to be tied down or to look for a career. Yet the fuller explanation is that this period of rootlessness was also a partial reflection of his own shortcomings. Sometimes he sought to establish his footing in a career but was unable or unwilling to do so.

In 1971, while still in the National Guard, Bush applied to law school at the University of Texas. His application was rejected. Later that year, Bush flirted with the notion of running for the Texas legislature, even floating the possibility in the Houston newspapers. After discussing the idea with his father, he backed away.

Finally, in late 1972 George W. was admitted to Harvard Business School. He hadn't even told his parents he was applying. Instead, Jeb broke the news to their father as he was trying to defuse the "mano a mano" confrontation, apparently to show their father that George W. was not the ne'er-do-well he may have seemed.

George W. entered Harvard in the fall of 1973 and spent the next two years there studying management, finance, and the other elements of the school's curriculum. He stood out among his more buttoned-down classmates by chewing tobacco, wearing his National Guard jacket to class, and leading expeditions to the Hillbilly Ranch, a country-music bar in downtown Boston. Many of his classmates spent their time putting together résumés and applying to Wall

Street or to *Fortune* 500 companies. Bush had no interest in that
sort of career. He left business school with as few commitments as
when he entered and with as little a sense of what he wanted to do
in life.

On the spring break before he graduated, on his way to visit a
friend in Arizona, he passed through Midland, Texas, the town
where he had grown up. An old family friend encouraged him to
come back and start his own oil business there. Bush quickly took
to the idea and decided to move there in the fall.

He was once again following the path of his father: passing up
Wall Street, moving to Texas, hoping to make money in oil. The
summer after business school, George W. spent a month visiting
his parents in Beijing, where his father was now serving as the head
of the U.S. liaison office there. On July 6, 1975, George H. W. Bush
wrote in his diary: "Today is George's twenty-ninth birthday. He
is off to Midland, starting a little later in life than I did, but nevertheless starting out on what I hope will be a challenging new life
for him. He is able. If he gets his teeth into something semiperma-
nent or permanent, he will do just fine."

In the mid-1970s, Midland was recovering from a prolonged economic slump. Oil prices were shooting upward, thanks in part to
the impact of the Arab oil embargo. Once again, it made economic
sense to explore and to drill, much as it had when Bush's father
made his money there in the 1950s. George W. moved into a tiny
apartment and soon began to cultivate old-timers in the oil business, including his father's friends. He began as a land man, studying deeds and other records to see who owned the mineral rights
to various parcels of land.

He drove from courthouse to courthouse in West Texas, gaining a toehold in the business. In June 1977, he incorporated his own
company, whimsically calling it Arbusto, the Spanish word for "bush."
Over the following years, that name would eventually spawn a series
of jokes. When the company's explorations hit some dry holes, some
in the oil industry pronounced Bush's firm "Are-bust-o," meaning
"bust," as in "out of money." Meanwhile, Texas journalists noticed
that Spanish-English dictionaries give another English word for

arbusto—"shrub"—and the newspaper columnist Molly Ivins eventually turned "Shrub" into a lasting nickname for George W. Bush.

Before Arbusto had even commenced operations, Bush put the
oil business aside to try his hand at politics. Bush's grandfather and
father had both run for office in middle age, after having become
wealthy businessmen. George W. had no desire to wait so long. In
1977, George Mahon, the Democratic congressman representing
West Texas, announced that he was stepping down from the House
seat that he had held for more than four decades. Although Bush
had been back in Midland for less than two years, he announced
his campaign for the seat. He positioned himself as a defender of
Texas oil interests, denouncing the federal government, proclaim-
ing the virtues of private enterprise, supporting free trade and, above
all, deregulation of government controls in energy markets.

Bush campaigned hard, traversing the district for more than a
year. But he lost because he was not as experienced as he thought.
His Democratic opponent, Kent Hance, repeatedly painted Bush
as an outsider. He reminded audiences that Bush had gone to Andover and Yale. "We don't need someone from the Northeast telling
us what the problems are," said one Hance campaign ad. When
Bush, who was an avid jogger, put on a bland TV ad that showed
him jogging, Hance told voters, "The only time folks around here
go running is when somebody's chasing 'em."

Bush sought to defuse these attacks with a sense of humor. When
one critic said Bush was not a native Texan, he replied, "No, I was
not born in Texas because I wanted to be close to my mother on
that day." But he generally refrained from launching his own coun-
terattacks. The campaign taught him an important lesson about
politics: he vowed that he would play rougher in future campaigns.
He would not sit back and let his opponents define him but would
seek to define them first. Bush never lost another campaign.

The 1978 race left one other enduring legacy. Bush turned to a
young political operative in Austin named Karl Rove for some informal help, and Rove became Bush's closest political adviser for the
remainder of his career. The two men had first met briefly at the
Republican National Committee in Washington several years

earlier while Bush's father was serving as the RNC chairman and
Rove was the president of the College Republicans organization.
In the late 1970s, George H. W. Bush took on Rove as an adviser
in his campaign for the 1980 Republican presidential nomination. But Rove also assisted George W.'s congressional race from a
distance, and they became good friends and allies: Rove was much
closer, in age and way of thinking, to George W. than to his father.

. . .

Bush remained single and unattached through his twenties. But in
the late 1970s, his personal life altered dramatically. The changes
started in 1976, soon after he turned thirty. He had gone out with a
group that included the tennis star John Newcombe near the family
vacation home in Kennebunkport, Maine, and locked into a prolonged drinking contest. While driving home, he was stopped by a
local policeman who discovered that Bush was unable to walk in a
straight line. He was charged with driving under the influence of
alcohol and pleaded guilty. Bush took this as a sign that it was time
for him to settle down. At a party in Texas the following summer,
his friends introduced him to Laura Welch, a librarian working in
Austin who had also grown up in Midland. Bush asked her out
to play miniature golf the following day and began to commute to
Austin to see her. They were married within four months in a small
ceremony in Midland. Four years later, Laura gave birth to twin daughters, Barbara and Jenna.

His choice of a spouse was revealing. Laura came from the town
where he grew up; she had no connection to any of the elite institutions where he had gone to school nor to the spheres of politics
or business in which he spent most of his working days. She was
also considerably more reserved and humble than his mother.
Indeed, for the first decade after their marriage, Laura considered
Barbara Bush to be distant, imperious, occasionally insulting, and
"ferociously tart-tongued."

Following his failed congressional race, Bush turned his energies
to his fledgling oil venture. He raised several million dollars for
Arbusto, relying heavily on the contacts of his uncle Jonathan Bush,

a money manager with extensive ties to Wall Street and Greenwich. In 1982, he renamed his company Bush Exploration, a change that enabled him to capitalize more directly on the family name at a time when his father was serving as Ronald Reagan's vice president.

George W. kept on looking for a big strike, but he never found it. During the 1980s, the price of oil collapsed, leaving Midland a city adrift. A local bank folded; offices and vacation homes were left empty; luxury automobiles were returned to car lots. Laura Bush recalled how one popular bumper sticker in West Texas at the time said: "Please Lord, let there be another boom. I promise I won't piss it away next time." In 1984 Bush merged his company with Spectrum 7, a firm owned by William DeWitt Jr., the son of the owner of the Cincinnati Reds. Bush served as chairman of the new firm, with a staff of fifteen. Yet this new company was soon in worse shape than Arbusto or Bush Exploration, and in 1986 Bush and his partners sold out to Harken Energy Corp., a Texas firm, which kept him on the board of directors.

During Bush's decade in the oil business, his investors lost millions of dollars amid the slump in oil prices. In some instances, however, those who gave money to his businesses later received appointments in the Reagan and George H. W. Bush administrations. George W. himself did not lose financially, because he was doing business primarily with other people's money. He started Arbusto in 1976 with his own $15,000 investment. He finally left the business with $840,000.

Questions were later raised about how he left the business. In 1990, while he was still a board member and at a time when the stock price of Harken was falling, Bush sold his shares in the company, but he did not file the required forms disclosing this fact for eight months. His action triggered a formal Securities and Exchange Commission investigation of whether Bush had violated the rules governing insiders, but in the end the SEC closed the probe without taking any action against him.

For George W., as for his father, the oil business in Texas proved to be merely a stepping-stone, not a lifetime career. As he entered his forties, he was ready for something else.

2

The Rising Politician

The turning point in George W. Bush's life came in the mid-1980s, when during a two-year period he turned forty, gave up alcohol, and gravitated increasingly toward religion.

His driving-under-the-influence arrest ten years earlier had prompted him to get married and settle down but not yet to give up drinking. By Bush's own account, drinking had become a regular staple of his evenings: generally the "three B's of bourbon, beer, and B&B" [Benedictine and brandy]. "I was drinking routinely, with an occasional bender thrown in," he later acknowledged. It was not enough to disrupt his workdays, and he was usually able to burn off the impact of the alcohol by going out for a run. But his drinking had become an embarrassment. "When he'd poured enough, he could be a bore," his wife, Laura, recalled. At one polite dinner with his parents' friends in Maine, he froze the table conversation by asking one woman, "So, what is sex like after fifty?"

In the summer of 1986, George and Laura Bush and their closest friends decided to celebrate his fortieth birthday at the Broadmoor Hotel in Colorado Springs. He drank heavily well into the night and woke up the next morning with a severe hangover. Later that day, he told his wife he had decided he would never have another drink. Afterward, he admitted he "craved alcohol" for a while, and he began to eat more and more chocolate, thus requiring him to run even more often. But he kept his vow and stayed sober.

During this same period, Bush also turned toward religion, not the established Episcopalian beliefs of his parents but evangelical Christianity. The change started, he said, with a meeting in Kennebunkport with Billy Graham, a longtime friend of the Bush family, and with regular meetings of a Bible study group back home in Midland. Barbara Bush was less than pleased with her son's evangelism, at one point objecting when her son told her that only those who had accepted Christ as their savior could go to heaven.

These two changes were inherently personal in nature, and they have frequently been portrayed as a trade-off: Bush gave up drinking and took up religion. Yet to put it in this simplistic fashion misses the larger political context in which both changes occurred. A fuller explanation would be that George W. gave up drinking and took up evangelical religion at a time when his father was preparing to run for president.

In April 1985, a few months after Ronald Reagan's reelection, George H. W. Bush, who was then vice president, summoned his entire family to a gathering at Camp David. Before the assembled Bush clan, the political strategist Lee Atwater outlined plans for a presidential campaign in 1988. The family was put on notice that all of them could be subjected to scrutiny by the press or by rival campaigns.

Laura Bush later pointed to the imminence of his father's presidential campaign as one of the factors behind her husband's decision to quit drinking. One of George W.'s closest friends in Midland, Joe O'Neill, confirmed this point, noting that Bush "looked in the mirror and said, 'Some day, I might embarrass my father. It might get my dad in trouble.'"

George W.'s turn to evangelical religion took place against this same backdrop. During the 1980 and 1984 elections, Reagan had succeeded in winning over large numbers of evangelical Christians who had earlier supported President Jimmy Carter, a Democrat. Under Reagan, evangelical voters grew in influence, particularly within the Republican Party. On television, Christian leaders such as Pat Robertson, Jerry Falwell, and Jim Bakker gained a nationwide following. As vice president, George H. W. Bush tried to court

these evangelical leaders, but they remained mistrustful of his establishment leanings, and the vice president and his wife seemed similarly ill at ease with them. (At one point, Barbara Bush referred to
some evangelical leaders as "these fakes.")

Gradually, their eldest son took on a role within the Bush campaign as the contact person in dealing with the Christian right. A
former Assembly of God minister named Doug Wead, who had long
been close to Bakker, began sending unsolicited memos to the Bush
staff and Atwater about evangelicals as a voting bloc and about possible strategies for winning them over. Eventually, the vice president and his family decided to bring Wead on staff, where he was
assigned directly to George W. When he reported for work, George
W. told him, "You're mine. You report to me." Wead proceeded to
arrange meetings with evangelical groups and leaders, seeking to
persuade them to support George H. W. Bush instead of Pat Robertson, who had decided to run for president himself in 1988.

· · ·

The Bush family was at first uneasy about George H. W. Bush's
choice of Lee Atwater to run his 1988 presidential campaign. Atwater was a political pro who moved from candidate to candidate and
had no strong or long-standing ties to the vice president; indeed,
others in Atwater's consulting firm were working for a rival Republican presidential candidate, Jack Kemp. Upon first meeting Atwater, George W. and Jeb Bush expressed skepticism about how loyal
he would be.

"How do we know we can trust you?" George W. asked Atwater. Jeb Bush added, "What he means is, if someone throws a gre-
nade at our dad, we expect you to jump on it." Taken aback, Atwater
countered with an invitation: one of the Bush brothers should come
to Washington, D.C., to work alongside Atwater and observe what
he was doing. However casually this offer may have been made,
George W. decided to accept it. In 1987, he and his family packed
up and moved to Washington, leaving Midland for good.

Bush took an office near Atwater's at campaign headquarters
and, to his surprise, he and Atwater proceeded to become close

friends. Both men shared the view that politics was a rough business in which candidates had to attack their opponents without
mercy. Bush had no specific title or responsibilities; in his own
words, he served as a "loyalty enforcer." Reporters covering George
H. W. Bush's 1988 campaign portrayed George W. as a political
version of Sonny Corleone, the tempestuous son in *The Godfather*,
who was quick to act against perceived enemies. "Junior was the
Roman candle of the family, bright, a sparkler—and quick to burn
the fingers," wrote Richard Ben Cramer in his book *What It Takes*.
When *Newsweek* published a cover story on George H. W. Bush
with the belittling headline "The Wimp Factor," George W. called
the magazine to vent the family's collective anger. For a time, he
cut off the magazine's access to the vice president.

Under Atwater's tutelage, George H. W. Bush ran a negative,
mudslinging campaign against Democratic nominee Michael Duka-
kis and won the election easily. Afterward, with his parents moving into the White House, George W., Laura, and their daughters
returned to Texas, settling in a new home in Dallas.

At this point, George W. had no company to run; he was free
to find something new. He already had an idea in the back of his
mind: one of his former business partners, William DeWitt Jr., told
him late in the 1988 campaign that he had heard the Texas Rangers baseball team might be for sale. Bush didn't have enough money
to purchase the team on his own, but during his first months in
Dallas he assembled a group of investors, some of them from Texas
and others brought in by DeWitt from Cincinnati. By the spring of
1989, the deal was concluded: Bush became the new managing part-
ner for the Rangers. The investors paid $75 million for 86 percent
of the team; of this sum, Bush's own investment was $606,000.

For Bush, running the Rangers was a dream job. In childhood,
Bush had been a baseball card collector, a Willie Mays fan, and a
memorizer of baseball statistics. For the following five years, he
spent his days supervising the Rangers' business operations, including payroll, trades, salary negotiations, and the construction of a
new ballpark in Arlington. He let others handle the details while
he served as the public face of the team, promoting it to Rotary

Clubs and chambers of commerce throughout the state and representing it in dealing with other club owners and the baseball commissioner. He attended most of the team's home games, chatting with players, fans, vendors, and ticket takers. In the process, he gained visibility and favorable publicity throughout Texas.

He meanwhile kept a hand in the developments of his father's administration, even from 1,200 miles away. He was assigned his own Secret Service detail and spent Christmases at Camp David along with the rest of the Bush family. Soon after the 1988 election, he headed a small internal group called the Scrub Team, which vetted appointees to the new administration—once again playing the role of loyalty enforcer. Three years into George H. W. Bush's administration, when Republicans began to demand the ouster of John Sununu, the White House chief of staff, it was George W. who assumed the role of hatchet man. He flew to Washington, asked to meet Sununu, and informed him he was becoming a burden. Sununu delivered a letter of resignation to the president six days later.

Although he was regarded as the most volatile and unpredictable of the Bush children, George W. was also the one whom his parents most frequently brought into high-level politics and diplomacy. When former Soviet leader Mikhail Gorbachev visited Washington in the spring of 1992, for example, the exclusive White House dinner for him included just eight people: the president and first lady, Gorbachev and his wife, Secretary of State James Baker and his wife, National Security Adviser Brent Scowcroft—and George W. Bush.

When his father ran for reelection that year, George W. again played an influential role in the campaign. Once again, he courted the Christian Right as an important part of the Republican coalition. Lee Atwater had died of brain cancer in 1991, and without him the Bush reelection campaign lacked a senior strategist. The younger Bush tried to offer advice, at one point suggesting that his father dump Vice President Dan Quayle and instead name Secretary of Defense Dick Cheney as his running mate. George H. W. Bush wasn't willing to do this, but the idea of putting Cheney on the ticket was one to which George W. would return eight years later.

With an economy that seemed to be floundering, his father lost the 1992 election to Governor Bill Clinton of Arkansas. That defeat marked the abrupt end of George H. W. Bush's long political career. For more than a quarter century, George W. had helped with his father's campaigns and had been defined, over and over again, as George H. W. Bush's son. Now, at age forty-six, George W. could not play that role any more. "Watching a good man lose made 1992 one of the worst years of my life," he wrote many years later.

He learned some lessons from his father's defeat. George H. W. Bush had never managed to win over the right wing of the party, particularly the evangelicals. He had been viewed as an elitist, out of touch with ordinary people, more an East Coast blue blood than a Texan. He had alienated foreign-policy hawks by failing to press for the breakup of the Soviet Union; as a result, quite a few neo-conservatives supported Clinton in 1992, and a few even went to work for him. Worst of all, George H. W. Bush had raised taxes, after explicitly pledging not to do so. His son took note of these political mistakes and would eventually seek to rectify all of them.

• • •

It is commonly assumed that George W. Bush started to contemplate a career in politics only after his father's defeat. The record shows otherwise. It is more accurate to say that George W. kept his own long-held plans to run for office in check until his father had left the national stage. The results of the 1992 election, crushing though they were for the Bush family, also cleared the way for George W. to launch his own political career.

His business career had gone nowhere, and baseball was little more than a hobby. Politics was the field he knew best, the one he enjoyed most, and the one in which he had acquired the most experience. Even during the early days, when he was drinking and was struggling in business, he had held top-level jobs in political campaigns. He had run once for Congress on his own and had helped manage his father's campaigns, twice for vice president and twice for the presidency. He had been schooled directly by Atwater in the high and low arts of American politics.

There was no particular issue or ideology driving him to political life, but then, from his own viewpoint, there hadn't been for
his father, either, who began his career as a Goldwater conservative before turning into a moderate Republican. George W. thought
he could be at least as good at winning elections as his father if not
better. His father had risen to high office mostly through a series
of appointments and at election time often found himself out of
tune with the Republican grassroots. George W. Bush's identity as
a tough-talking Texan, his ties with evangelical groups and other
groups that had mistrusted his father—and still, on the other hand,
the Bush family name—all gave him the confidence that if he ran,
he would do well.

In early 1989, soon after his father's inauguration, George W.
had begun to flirt with the idea of running for governor of Texas
the following year. He spent several months traveling through the
state, talking to local Republican leaders and donors and generat-
ing a wave of news stories and magazine profiles about his possible
candidacy.

Among those opposing the idea was his mother. Barbara Bush
worried that if the two George Bushes, father and son, held office
at the same time, then any unpopular actions by either one of them
could drag down the other one. At one point, to her son's chagrin,
she said publicly that she thought he should devote his energy to
the baseball team he had just acquired. "When you make a major
commitment like that, I think maybe you won't be running for
governor," she told reporters.

Finally, in August 1989, George W. announced that he had
decided not to run, and for the next several years he occupied himself with the Texas Rangers. Bush himself later reflected that it was
in these baseball years that he learned how to become more comfortable as a public speaker. "I also gained valuable experience handling tough questions from journalists, in this case mostly about
our shaky pitching rotation," he recalled.

His ownership stake in the Rangers made him a wealthy man
for the first time in his life. With the construction of a new ballpark in Arlington and the growing popularity of the Rangers, Bush's

initial investment of $606,000 increased in value: by the time he sold his shares in the team in the late 1990s, they were worth $14.9 million.

By 1992, his father's final year in the White House, George W. seemed almost desperate to get started in his own political career and to overcome, finally, nicknames like Junior that identified him as his father's child. "I'm his kid, but I'm also older than his vice president," George W., then forty-five years old, admonished one reporter.

Within months after his father's defeat, he began preparing to run for governor of Texas once again, this time in earnest. The Democratic governor, Ann Richards, was up for reelection in 1994. Richards was an old adversary of the Bush family: in a speech to the 1988 Democratic National Convention, she had delivered the famous quip that George H. W. Bush was "born with a silver foot in his mouth." She was flamboyant, acid-tongued, and by all appearances extremely popular in Texas.

Nevertheless, George W. decided to try to unseat her. He ran his first statewide campaign hand in hand with his old friend Karl Rove, who had become a notable political consultant in Texas. Both men had studied the campaign techniques of Lee Atwater. Bush also hired a former Texas television reporter, Karen Hughes, to serve as his communications director, and she quickly became part of the Bush inner circle.

It was in Bush's 1994 gubernatorial race that he and Rove came up with their disciplined strategy: Bush should keep his temper in check, concentrate on a few broad themes, avoid getting sidetracked, and hold relentlessly to the same messages and response lines throughout the long campaign. Years later, Richards recalled with a mix of frustration and admiration how difficult it had been to engage Bush: "I think that the talent that George Bush has—and I say this with real respect—is that rather than tell you the intricacies of what he knows or what he intends to do, he is very good at saying things that are rather all-encompassing. You know, if you said to George, 'What time is it?' he would say, 'We must teach our children to read.'"

Education was one of the issues Bush chose to emphasize in the campaign. Richards had endorsed the idea of transferring some money from wealthier school districts to poorer districts. That gave Bush a chance to argue that although she was a witty, engaging personality, her actual policies were out of touch with conservative, middle-class Texans. Bush promised repeatedly to transfer more control over public schools to local districts. He also pledged to improve the criminal justice system, renew efforts to alleviate poverty, overhaul welfare, and institute tort reform.

Bush felt a pressing need to establish his own political identity, separate from that of his father. He had never held public office, and memories of George H. W. Bush's White House years were fresh. "All that I ask is that for once, you guys stop seeing me as the son of George Bush," he told an interviewer in 1994. "This campaign is about me, no one else."

This problem was further compounded by the fact that his brother Jeb was running that year for governor of Florida, so that there were, inevitably, national news stories juxtaposing the two Bush sons and their political ambitions. George W. repeatedly sought to downplay the family connection. His father did not appear beside him during the campaign, and George W. did not mention his father in campaign appearances.

Richards portrayed Bush as a lightweight who was inexperienced in government. She dubbed him Prince George or George the Younger. During her campaign, she pointed to his lack of success in business, described the financial help he got from family and friends, criticized the use of public funds to build a new ballpark for the Rangers, and brought up the Securities and Exchange Commission investigation of his sale of Harken stock.

She tried to provoke Bush and to rattle him. On the night of the only television debate of the campaign, Richards and Bush accidentally met on a hotel elevator. She looked at him and said, "This one's going to be tough on you, boy." Yet Bush maintained his equipoise, both in the debate and throughout the extended campaign, leaving it to Rove and other aides to attack Richards. They pointed to the campaign contributions Richards was receiving from Holly-

wood and from national liberal organizations as proof that she was
somehow less Texan than Bush.

Meanwhile, Bush worked hard to court the conservatives and
the evangelicals whose lack of support had so badly damaged his
father in 1992. He invited radio talk-show host Rush Limbaugh to
be his guest at the Texas Rangers game marking Nolan Ryan's retirement. The month before Election Day, the *Houston Post* reported
that Bush, in an interview, said he believed that "heaven is only open
to those who accept Jesus Christ."

During the final weeks of the campaign, Ross Perot, the Texas
businessman whose independent presidential campaign in 1992 had
cost George H. W. Bush the election, endorsed Richards: one Bush
family nemesis lining up behind another. It didn't matter. Although
Richards had originally been the favorite, Bush captured 53 percent of the electorate, a margin of more than 300,000 votes.

The nationwide results that November included a second development of profound consequence for George W.: in Florida, his
brother Jeb was defeated. That meant that George W. suddenly
became the leading political figure in the Bush family, the one who
was gaining the experience necessary to run for president. Even
when Jeb Bush won in his second race for governor in 1998, he
was not on an equal footing with his older brother.

· · ·

As governor of Texas, Bush tried out some of the same ideas, arguments, and catchphrases he would later use as president. It was in
Texas that Bush first called himself a "compassionate conservative,"
a slogan his father's political advisers had come up with during the
1988 presidential campaign. It was during his years as governor that
Bush first proposed "faith-based" initiatives, in which governments
could turn to religious organizations to provide social services. It was
in Texas that Bush first emphasized the importance of requiring
elementary-school students to pass basic standardized tests for
reading and other basic skills. Even some of the one-liners Bush used
as president were taken directly from his time as governor. "I've
got a lot of capital to spend, and I'm going to spend every dime of

it," he once observed in Texas, with virtually the same words he, would use after winning reelection as president in 2004.

Nevertheless, Bush's performance as governor stands out in hindsight because of the contrast with his more confrontational approach and his more sweeping and ambitious policies as president. In Texas, he often sought to avoid conflict and to portray himself as a moderate Republican. He formed close relationships with the Democratic leaders of the Texas legislature. He often proved willing to compromise to get his programs enacted.

During his first year in office, Bush won approval for greater control for local school districts. He also succeeded in implementing changes to Texas's juvenile justice system, tort laws, and welfare requirements, each of which he had cited as priorities during the 1994 campaign. Bush formed an unusually tight bond with Bob Bullock, the Democratic lieutenant governor, a feisty old-style politician and the state's most powerful figure. (In Texas, the lieutenant governor is elected separately from the governor and has enormous power over the Texas Senate, serving as its president and determining its agenda.) Bush courted Bullock so assiduously that Bullock later crossed party lines to endorse Bush for president.

On social issues, Governor Bush occasionally proved to be surprisingly liberal. In 1996, a federal appeals court struck down as unconstitutional an affirmative-action program in which the University of Texas had set aside specific places in its law school for members of minority groups. In response, Bush signed a law that required public colleges and universities in Texas to admit any student who graduated in the top 10 percent of his or her high school class. That measure, widely praised by civil rights leaders, ensured that the best black and Hispanic students from largely segregated schools could gain admission to the state university system, even if their standardized test scores were lower than those of whites elsewhere. "We want all our students in Texas to have a fair shot at achieving their dreams," said Bush in signing the bill.

He refused to join in the growing backlash within the Republican Party against immigration. In California, Governor Pete Wilson strongly endorsed a ballot measure that denied state benefits to illegal aliens, but Bush refused to support Wilson's approach. Indeed, in his campaigns for governor and as president, Bush consistently won greater percentages of Latino votes than other Republican candidates.

As governor of Texas, Bush was not a radical tax cutter in the way that he later became as president. When Bush proposed cutting property taxes, he sought to offset some of the losses to the state treasury by increasing sales and business taxes. In the process, he aroused the ire of antitax conservatives, who said he had violated a promise not to raise taxes. The Texas legislature eventually rejected his proposals to change the tax laws.

On crime and the death penalty, he remained staunchly conservative. Texas executes more death-row inmates than any other state, and in the Bush years the frequency increased. There were 152 executions during Bush's six years in office, each one approved by the governor. He granted clemency only once. At one point, Christian groups pleaded with Bush to block the execution of Karla Faye Tucker, a convicted murderer who had converted to Christianity while in prison. Bush turned down their appeals. On another occasion, a Canadian citizen convicted of murder was given a death sentence. After Canadian officials protested, Bush told reporters, "If you're Canadian and you come to our state, don't murder anybody."

Politically, the details of Bush's performance as governor did not matter all that much. His name was Bush and he was the Republican governor of the nation's second-largest state; those facts alone made him a likely presidential contender. Later, after he won the Republican presidential nomination, a reporter asked his father to explain George W.'s rapid ascent. The former president replied that once his son became governor of Texas, "It's a six-inch putt."

· · ·

The planning for a presidential campaign started early, after Bush had been governor for little more than a year. In the early spring of 1996, soon after Bob Dole wrapped up the Republican nomination, Rove began talking to Bush about running in 2000 and discovered that Bush himself had already begun to think about it. Both of them calculated that Dole would lose, and that the Republicans would turn to a younger candidate four years later. Indeed, Bush thought that one important factor in his father's loss to Bill Clinton had been the generational difference between them: America's baby-boom generation was beginning to dominate American politics and was turning toward leaders of its own.

At the 1996 Republican National Convention, Rove worked on Bush's behalf, arranging interviews for reporters who wanted to write profiles of him and telling Republican delegates that the governor of Texas was "our Clinton." After Dole lost the election, reporters and handicappers quickly put Bush on their short lists of potential Republican candidates for 2000. The other contenders were, as a group, not formidable; each seemed to have defects. Colin Powell had no strong desire to run and was too liberal for the party's base. Jack Kemp was conservative but had never been elected to anything beyond a House seat. Dan Quayle could never overcome his image as lacking in gravitas.

Over the following two years Rove, by his own account, "was constantly plotting, planning and scheming" on Bush's behalf. Bush, meanwhile, devoted much of his energy to winning reelection as governor of Texas. He and Rove began lining up a nationwide network of donors, many of whom had previously supported George H. W. Bush's campaigns. In 1998 the Bush-Rove team put special emphasis on winning Hispanic support in places like El Paso that had historically supported Democratic candidates. The goal, in both cases, was not just to win reelection in Texas but also to demonstrate to Republicans elsewhere that Bush would be a strong national candidate.

These efforts were largely successful. Bush defeated his Democratic opponent Garry Mauro in a landslide: 68 percent to 31 percent. The demographics of Bush's support were even more impressive: he won 49 percent of the Hispanic vote, 65 percent of women, and 70 percent of political independents.

After such a convincing reelection, Bush became not just a leading candidate for the Republication nomination but the favorite.

"The race is his to lose," declared the conservative *National Review* only days after the 1998 results came in. A *Washington Post* poll taken in March 1999 found that 52 percent of registered Republican voters said they would vote for Bush. These promising early polls enabled Bush to raise unprecedented sums of money. The Bush campaign developed and refined the then novel fund-raising technique of "bundling." Instead of having the campaign seek donations one by one, the Bush team asked key supporters to raise money from their families, friends, business associates, and former classmates. The top fund-raisers, called Pioneers, each raised $100,000 or more. The result was that in the year 1999 alone, the Bush campaign took in nearly $70 million, far more than any other candidate.

Bush's fund-raising prowess deterred some candidates from declaring for the presidency and pushed others out of the race. In April 1999 Kemp announced that he would not run. In September, Quayle, who had declared his candidacy earlier in the year, dropped out, saying he couldn't raise enough money to compete. In October, Elizabeth Dole quit, too. "The bottom line remains money," she explained.

Bush did not formally declare his own candidacy until June 1999. But the reality was that he had been carefully putting together his team and organization for more than a year. His father also played a crucial role. In August 1998, the former president invited one of his former national security aides, Condoleezza Rice, to the family compound at Kennebunkport for a weekend at a time when George W. was also visiting. That weekend, Bush and Rice spent time together, just as his father hoped they would. Bush told her that he was thinking of running for president. They talked about sports (Rice, like Bush, was an avid sports fan) and about her upbringing in segregated Birmingham. But Rice also began to talk to Bush about foreign policy, starting to prepare him for what he might need to know in a campaign. She found him "funny and irreverent, but serious about policy." Bush soon picked Rice as his principal campaign adviser on foreign policy. Over the following year, Rice helped put together a small advisory group of other former officials, all of them veterans of past Republican administrations.

On a whim, this group called itself the Vulcans, a reference to the Roman god of the forge, who is immortalized in a huge statue in Rice's hometown of Birmingham.

Bush and Rove similarly put together an economic team composed in large part of former officials from past Republican administrations, a group headed by economist Lawrence Lindsey. A former Federal Reserve official, Lindsey was a devotee of supply-side economics, the tax-cutting philosophy embraced by Ronald Reagan that George H. W. Bush had once dismissively derided as "voodoo economics." At the beginning of his presidential campaign, George W. Bush endorsed a proposal for a sizable tax cut.

Thus, by the beginning of 2000, as the candidates entered the primaries, Bush had adroitly managed to win support across the spectrum of Republican Party politics. He was the favored candidate of the Wall Street establishment and of moderate Republicans, inheriting his father's supporters and donors. His proposed tax cut appealed to economic conservatives. He maintained the amicable ties with social conservatives and the Christian Right that he had forged during his father's 1988 campaign and deepened during his years in Texas. By appealing to these disparate constituencies, Bush held the Republicans' intraparty bickering to a minimum. In the process, however, he drove the Republican Party considerably further to the right than it had been during his father's administration.

The only opponent who mounted a serious primary challenge to Bush was Senator John McCain of Arizona, who had won a reputation as a maverick legislator willing to challenge special interests. McCain attracted support from party reformers and from some moderate Republicans and independents. He was also the favorite candidate of the party's neoconservatives: the foreign-policy hawks, many of them former Democrats, who had supported Ronald Reagan because of his anticommunist views. At the time of the 2000 primaries, Bush's views on foreign policy were barely formed, and the neoconservatives had for years mistrusted his father. By contrast, McCain, a former Vietnam prisoner of war whose father and grandfather were admirals, supported an assertive American role overseas.

In January 2000, Bush won the Iowa caucuses, a contest in which McCain did not compete. Instead, McCain allocated virtually all of his time, energy, and money to defeating Bush in the New Hampshire primary one week later. Taking the attack, McCain repeatedly criticized Bush's proposal for a large tax cut. McCain argued that the Bush tax plan would hurt low- and middle-income Americans and put the Social Security trust fund in danger. One McCain television advertisement said that Bush would "take every last dime of the surplus and spend it on tax cuts that mostly benefit the wealthy." McCain won New Hampshire overwhelmingly, with 49 percent of the vote to Bush's 30 percent.

That set up an epic showdown between Bush and McCain in South Carolina. In at least one instance, a Bush supporter sent out a scurrilous email saying that McCain "chose to sire children without marriage," adding that one of those children was not white. (The truth was that McCain and his wife, Cindy, had adopted a child from Bangladesh.) Rove has long maintained that he and the Bush campaign had nothing to do with these tactics, which were said to be the work of individual supporters. The acrimony became so great that, after one debate, Bush put his arm around McCain and said he had nothing to do with the slander campaign against him. McCain retorted, "Don't give me that shit. And take your hands off me."

In the end, South Carolina went for Bush, who won 53 percent of the vote to McCain's 42 percent. With that result, Bush effectively won the Republican nomination. McCain did not have the money or organization for a prolonged, nationwide battle. Two weeks after South Carolina, Bush won nine of thirteen primaries, including California, New York, and Ohio, and McCain withdrew from the race. Nonetheless, it took McCain two months to endorse Bush, before finally campaigning with him against the Democrats in the fall.

· · ·

Bush devoted the next seven months to his general-election campaign against Vice President Al Gore, who had easily won the Democratic nomination. Bush's principal campaign issue was not one of policy but of character: the Monica Lewinsky scandal was still fresh, and Bush promised voters that he would "restore honor and dignity" to the White House. Bush pressed Gore to tell voters whether he approved of Bill Clinton's conduct. Gore handled the issue awkwardly, offering conflicting messages and keeping his distance from the president.

Despite his family lineage, his wealth, and his elite education, Bush skillfully presented himself to voters as an ordinary, down-to-earth person, one who was more in touch with their daily lives than Gore, who came across as wooden. On his campaign plane, Bush sometimes charmed reporters with his love of nicknames and his self-deprecating jokes. He mangled words and phrases with regularity: he called the Greeks the "Grecians" and once voiced sympathy for voters struggling to "put food on their family." Yet he made light of his mistakes. At the start of his campaign, he took his plane's public-address system to tell reporters traveling with him, "Please stow your expectations securely in your overhead bins." On the final flight before Election Day, he announced, "Last chance for malaprops."

In July, Bush made the most important decision of the campaign, one that would determine the course, the policies, and indeed the very character of his future administration. Bush appointed Dick Cheney, his father's former secretary of defense, to search for and vet the possible candidates to be his running mate. Cheney compiled dossiers on a long list of current or former senators and governors. Each one was required to fill out extensive questionnaires on their financial holdings and personal life, and to submit to rigorous interviews by Cheney. However, while the process was still under way, Bush decided he wanted Cheney himself.

Rove resisted. He contended that in political terms Cheney would do little to help Bush's chances of election; his home state of Wyoming had only three electoral votes and was reliably Republican. Rove also noted that Cheney had health issues and an extensive conservative voting record in Congress, one that Democrats would attack. Finally, he argued that the selection of Cheney would revive criticisms that George W. Bush represented merely a restoration of the George H. W. Bush administration.

Yet at this juncture, continuity with his father's administration was precisely what George W. Bush seemed to want and to need. He chose Cheney not to win the election but to help him govern afterward. He wanted a vice president who knew the internal workings and processes of the federal government. Cheney, who had served not only as secretary of defense but also as White House chief of staff in the Ford administration and as House minority whip, possessed experience that no other candidate could match. George H. W. Bush appears to have played an important role behind the scenes, much as he did in introducing his son to Condoleezza Rice. He told his son that Cheney would be "a great choice."

The selection of Cheney had an impact that was tinged with irony: seeking continuity with his father's administration, Bush unintentionally opened the way for a shift away from it. During the George H. W. Bush administration, Cheney's strong conservatism had been counterbalanced by other figures such as National Security Adviser Brent Scowcroft and Colin Powell, the chairman of the Joint Chiefs of Staff. However, as George W. Bush's vice president, Cheney would hold higher rank and greater authority to propagate his own deeply held views of American power.

In advance of the fall debates, the campaign team worried about how Bush would perform. They sought to handle the problem by lowering expectations, pointing reporters to a magazine article that portrayed Gore as an experienced debater who had easily handled any opponent who came his way. The ploy worked; in dealing with Gore, Bush simply held his ground and avoided any major gaffes. The coverage of the debates focused more on Gore's idiosyncrasies: he sighed frequently in one debate, was overly made up in another, and sometimes came across as overbearing or patronizing. There was one moment that was little noticed at the time but took on greater significance years later. Asked about America's role in the world, Bush emphasized, above all, the importance of humility. "If we're an arrogant nation, they'll view us that way, but if we're a humble nation, they'll respect us," he answered.

In late October, immediately after the final presidential debate, surveys showed that Bush led by a substantial margin, in some national polls by as much as 10 percentage points. Then the lead suddenly slipped away. On the Thursday before the election, the story broke about Bush's 1976 arrest in Kennebunkport, Maine, for driving under the influence of alcohol.

For the Bush campaign, this was not merely some long-forgotten episode. Bush had already discussed with his closest aides how to handle the DUI case, if it were to come to light. They had even considered disclosing it on their own in some nonsensational manner. Instead, they had decided to keep it secret. The incident had taken place not in Texas but in Maine, where reporters and political opponents would be less likely to search the records.

Pressed by reporters, Bush responded with an updated version of his old standard campaign line that he had been irresponsible in his youth. "I've often times said that years ago, I made some mistakes. I occasionally drank too much," he told reporters. He was helped by the fact that the incident was not reported until five days before the election and therefore was given much less coverage than it would have been accorded earlier in the campaign; a Bush friend phoned John Newcombe in Sydney, Australia, and he went into hiding to avoid any inquiries from the press.

Nevertheless, the DUI story did hurt Bush. In the final days and hours of the campaign, the Bush team found itself on the defensive, answering questions about his past drinking: had he really quit, had he been arrested elsewhere? The revelation also seemed to conflict with the broader themes of honesty and virtue on which Bush had based his entire presidential campaign. "It was jarring for people to hear him admit he'd been arrested," Rove acknowledged years later. "Many Americans had been drawn by his pledge to restore integrity to the Oval Office, and now he had surprised them with a DUI."

On Election Night, using exit polls and early returns, the television networks began to tabulate and call the fifty states for either Bush or Gore. One of the earliest states where the results seemed clear was Florida, which NBC called for Gore at 7:49 p.m. CBS and ABC quickly followed suit. Over the following two hours, the networks reported that Gore had won enough states that he needed only one more to win the election. Shortly before 10 p.m., Gore won New Mexico, and the networks began to call the entire election for Gore.

But then, the Bush and Gore camps and the networks all began to get phone calls from Florida telling them that the vote there seemed extremely close, contrary to the networks' earlier reports. As a result, Florida was shifted back into the undecided category, leaving the election still open. Shortly after 2:00 a.m., first Fox News and then the other networks switched ground and called Florida for Bush, announcing that he had won the presidency.

Minutes later, Gore telephoned Bush at the governor's mansion in Austin to concede the election. The vice president then left his hotel for Nashville's War Memorial Plaza to deliver a concession speech. Just as Gore was heading to the podium, aides held him back. The returns from Florida were so close that the situation appeared to qualify for a mandatory recount, they told him. The election was not over yet. Gore phoned Bush back. "Circumstances have changed since I first called you," the vice president said.

"Are you saying what I think you're saying?" asked Bush. "Let me make sure that I understand. You're calling back to retract that concession?" Bush told Gore his "little brother" Jeb, the governor of Florida, had assured him that he had won the state.

What followed was without precedent in American history: a thirty-six-day battle in the courts over the election results. It bounced from courthouse to courthouse and, in Florida, from county to county, as lawyers debated the question of who should be awarded that state's electoral votes and thus be declared president of the United States. The Gore team dispatched a former secretary of state, Warren Christopher, to direct its challenge to the vote tallies in Florida. The Bush campaign countered with another former secretary of state, James Baker, for decades a close friend of the Bush family.

Immediately after Election Day, the official tallies showed that Bush had a margin of fewer than two thousand votes in Florida out of 5.8 million votes cast. Throughout the long postelection dispute, Baker and his team argued repeatedly that this ballot should be considered official, while Gore and Christopher contended that there were irregularities in the voting that necessitated a recount.

Gore played an active role in directing the legal battle. Bush, in contrast, stayed detached and left virtually all the decision making up to Baker. He appeared in public occasionally in an effort to show that he was already preparing to take office. But Bush spent most of his time at his own ranch in Crawford, Texas, a place so secluded it had no cable or satellite television.

The Florida Supreme Court, dominated by Democratic judicial appointees, twice ruled for Gore, ordering a manual recount of those ballots for which no vote for president had been recorded. Ordinarily, such decisions would be final; the Florida Supreme Court was a state court, ruling on a question of state law, and the U.S. Supreme Court does not generally get involved in such disputes. Indeed, the conservative Supreme Court headed by Chief Justice William H. Rehnquist had issued a series of significant decisions on federalism that had emphasized its reluctance to intrude on the authority of state courts.

However, in this case, which became known to history as *Bush v. Gore*, the U.S. Supreme Court decided to intervene in the case to hear claims that the Florida Supreme Court was violating the U.S. Constitution by ordering a recount. On December 12, 2000, the justices voted five to four to overturn the Florida court rulings. The effect of the Supreme Court's action was to allow the official tally certified by Florida's Republican secretary of state to stand. Bush was declared the winner of Florida's electoral votes.

With that U.S. Supreme Court decision the election was over. Seven weeks after Election Day, Bush became the president-elect, even though Gore had won the popular vote. Once again, Gore called Bush to concede. This time, Gore afterward stepped before cameras to say that he had made the momentous phone call, adding: "And I promised him that I wouldn't call him back this time." Within four days, Bush began making his cabinet appointments, starting with his choice for secretary of state, Colin Powell.

The Bush-Gore race and the prolonged postelection controversy had an impact on the Bush presidency that was profound and enduring. The battle left both Bush and his Democratic opponents with a series of misimpressions that would be damaging, in various ways, to each side.

The Democrats believed that Bush, having won such a narrow and disputed victory, would need to move to the center. In order to govern, they reasoned, Bush would need to moderate his views and become more conciliatory. They were not prepared to deal with a new president who would prove to be both bold in his initiatives and highly partisan in his approach.

Bush came to office with his own serious misconceptions. From the long campaign and its aftermath, he derived the impression that he did not need to have any deep grasp of policy or of history because he could rely heavily on his advisers, including, above all, his father's advisers. Bush had done little more during the campaign than to come up with some phrases or brushstrokes for what he might do in office. He had told voters his own lack of experience didn't matter, because he possessed an experienced group of aides to assist him. He had persuaded himself that there would always be someone around whom he could trust and to whom he could delegate responsibility, as he had with Baker in Florida.

It had not occurred to Bush yet that his advisers might not agree among themselves, that there might be submerged but intense frictions among them whose resolution would require more knowledge and experience than he possessed. Nor did George W. Bush realize that he would soon face world-changing events unlike any that his father's administration had ever confronted. He was a president with a bold domestic agenda, lacking majority support among the American public and confronting a world for which neither he nor his famous advisers were prepared.

3

———

The New President and
His Tax Cuts

On January 20, 2001, thirty-nine days after the Supreme Court decision, George W. Bush was sworn in as the nation's forty-third president. As he took the oath of office, his father brushed back tears; the two of them became the first father-and-son pair to serve as president since John Adams and John Quincy Adams. In his inaugural address, the younger Bush called upon the nation to rise above the rancor of the 2000 campaign and its aftermath. "Civility is not a tactic or a sentiment," he declared. "It is the determined choice of trust over cynicism, of community over chaos."

There were widespread expectations that after the bitterly fought election, Bush would begin modestly and seek reconciliation with the Democrats. Those predictions were based on the notion that he would need to broaden his political support in order to govern. He had become president without winning a majority of the popular vote, and the election had resulted in a Senate that was split, fifty to fifty, and a House of Representatives in which Republicans held only a narrow majority of nine seats. A patient, accommodating approach would have been in accordance with the way Bush, as governor, had courted the support of Democratic leaders in the Texas legislature. Furthermore, his presidency had a hurried startup: the delays in settling the 2000 election prompted by *Bush v. Gore* meant that Bush took office with an unusually short transition period.

Bush confounded all these predictions. During his first months, he put forward far-reaching initiatives and took a hard line in pressing for them. Indeed, the most consequential piece of domestic legislation in Bush's entire tenure in the White House was enacted less than five months after he took office. It was called the Economic Growth and Tax Relief Reconciliation Act of 2001, more commonly known as the first of the Bush tax cuts. That measure, followed by another major tax reduction two years later, would effectively transform America's economy, its politics, and, indeed, the very nature of American society.

Bush had made his promise to cut taxes the centerpiece of his 2000 campaign. At the time, this pledge served the purpose of undercutting Steve Forbes, the antitax Republican who had run as the conservative alternative to Bob Dole in the 1996 primaries and had announced his candidacy for 2000. More important, Bush's campaign proposal, which called for a reduction of $1.6 trillion over a ten-year period, served notice to the right wing of the Republican Party that he would govern differently from his father. Conservatives had never forgiven the elder Bush for raising taxes a decade earlier.

In the final years of the Clinton administration, the U.S. government had begun to run growing budget surpluses, the result of America's growing prosperity and a tax increase in the early Clinton years. By 2000 it was estimated that over the following decade, the surpluses would add up to $4.6 trillion. At one point in that year's presidential campaign, Bush accused Al Gore, his Democratic opponent, of making so many promises to voters that he would fritter away the surplus.

By early 2001, as Bush took office, there was considerable debate over what to do with the surplus. The nation could spend more on new programs, such as education, health care, or infrastructure; it could use the surplus to pay down America's long-term debt; or it could return the money to taxpayers in the form of a rebate or a tax cut.

Bush took the latter course, urging Congress to enact the tax cuts he had proposed during the campaign and to do so quickly.

His underlying rationale was simple. "I believed government was taking too much of the people's money," he later explained. Bush called for a series of reductions in the personal income tax across all brackets, but the most significant proposal was to drop the rate for the highest tax bracket from 39 percent to 33 percent. He also advocated the abolition of estate taxes. Under the plan Bush submitted to Congress more than a third of all the tax savings was to go to the top 1 percent of all taxpayers.

Less than a week after Bush's swearing-in, Alan Greenspan, the chairman of the Federal Reserve, supported the idea of a tax cut, testifying that the large surpluses made cutting taxes a reasonable approach. Greenspan included the proviso that such a cut should be conditional: if the surplus vanished, the tax cuts should end, too. Greenspan's endorsement carried enormous impact, but the conditionality was accorded far less attention.

Bush's plan quickly ran into resistance from Democratic leaders, from a handful of moderate Republicans, and from his own secretary of the treasury, Paul O'Neill. The Democrats protested that the cuts were skewed toward higher-income Americans and would reduce the money available for social programs. O'Neill, a longtime friend of both Cheney and Greenspan, strongly opposed the idea of a permanent tax cut, arguing instead that the legislation should include "triggers" that would end or phase out the tax reductions if the federal government began running deficits once again.

Bush's justification for the tax cuts changed over time. Initially, the rationale was that the nation was running a large budget surplus, but later on his argument was that because the economy was sliding toward recession, a tax cut was needed to stimulate spending. O'Neill countered that if boosting the economy were the objective, then a better response would be to give taxpayers a large, onetime rebate that would put money into immediate circulation, without fixing into law a tax cut that would affect the economy and the government's budgets years into the future. "I have about $125 billion of surplus in Treasury's checking account," O'Neill told one group of senators. "Why don't you use that for an immediate tax rebate?"

Bush held firm. In this initial battle, he displayed many of the qualities that would come to characterize his presidency. He refused to let the debate become bogged down in nuances or detail, such as the idea of "triggers." He formulated a simple position and tried to hold to it. When his economic advisers began suggesting in March that he scale back his proposals, Bush replied, "It's not time to negotiate. We'll be negotiating with ourselves." A variant of this line—*I'm not going to negotiate against myself*—became a frequent Bush refrain.

Rather than seeking a compromise, Bush managed to persuade quite a few conservative and centrist Democrats to support his proposals. The overall size of the tax-cut package was cut from $1.6 trillion to $1.35 trillion over ten years, and the reduction in the top income tax rates was fixed at 35 percent rather than 33 percent. The estate tax was not abolished, but the amounts excluded from the tax were steadily increased, and the tax rate itself was cut.

Finally, sunset provisions were written into the legislation, so that the tax cuts would expire after ten years. This time limit served to keep the tax package in compliance with a Senate rule that had set limits on how much the federal deficit could be increased. It made the tax package seem less costly and thus more palatable. Yet in practical terms, as supporters realized, the tax cuts would be difficult to reverse. After Bush left the White House, his successor was obliged to wage a two-year campaign to persuade Congress to let the Bush tax cuts expire as planned under the sunset provisions and then only for those with high incomes; the tax cuts for the middle class proved politically untouchable and were made permanent, adding considerably to the budget deficit.

Bush's initial legislative battle had a series of profound political ramifications, both immediately and over the long run. During the negotiations on the tax bill, a group of moderate Republican senators tried unsuccessfully to persuade Bush to water down the legislation. One of them, Senator James Jeffords of Vermont, asked Bush to allot more money to special education. When Bush turned him down, Jeffords quit the Republican Party and became an independent who caucused with the Democrats, thereby giving the

Democrats control of the Senate until the next congressional election. "In the past, the various wings of the Republican Party in Congress have had some freedom to argue and influence and ultimately
to shape the party's agenda," Jeffords told reporters. "The election
of President Bush changed that dramatically." Jeffords's defection
presaged a broader change. Under Bush, the center of gravity within
the Republican Party shifted steadily to the right, and moderates
were increasingly marginalized.

Bush followed up these initial tax reductions with another round
of sizable cuts two years later. By then, the hopes in early 2001 of
budget surpluses extending through the end of the decade were all
but forgotten; the federal government was already running a deficit, and the only question was the extent to which any new tax cut
would increase that deficit. Just after the 2002 elections, during
his final month in office, O'Neill argued against new tax cuts on
grounds that the federal government was already moving toward
fiscal crisis. However, Cheney told him, "Reagan proved deficits
don't matter. . . . We won the midterms. This is our due."

This time, Bush at first proposed a complete elimination of taxes
on dividends as part of a package of $550 billion in new cuts. There
was stronger opposition in Congress than in 2001, both because of
the mounting budget deficits and because of Democratic criticisms
that the package was skewed toward the wealthy. There are some
indications that by this juncture Bush himself was becoming uneasy
with how much his actions were helping people in the highest tax
brackets. During the discussions over his package, he asked at one
point: "Won't the top-rate people benefit the most from eliminat-
ing the double taxation of dividends? Didn't we already give them
a break at the top?"

By the time of the second tax cut, Bush had already dispatched
American troops to Iraq. That made the tax cuts of 2003 historic:
in every other military conflict since the Civil War, U.S. presidents
have raised taxes to help defray the costs. Bush not only declined
to raise taxes during wartime but lowered them. When one of Bush's
principal economic advisers, Lawrence Lindsey, speculated before
the Iraq War that it would cost more than $100 billion, the White

House repudiated his prediction, and Bush fired him two months later. Lindsey's estimate turned out to be far too low.

Ultimately, Congress decided not to abolish the tax on dividends but instead to cut the top tax rate to 15 percent. It also cut the maximum tax on capital gains to the same rate of 15 percent. The size of the package was cut from $550 billion to $350 billion. This measure passed the House 231 to 200, with only seven Democrats supporting the measure. The Senate divided fifty to fifty. Cheney, who as vice president presided over the Senate, cast the final vote necessary for passage.

These reductions in taxes on dividends and capital gains created new pools of wealth for upper-income Americans and widened the gulf between rich and poor. The economy, which had been in recession during Bush's first year in office, started to revive in 2003, but economists began to speak of a "two-tier recovery," with a surge of new consumption of luxury goods and much more modest growth for middle- and lower-income Americans. Sales of $600-a-night luxury hotel suites and $5,000 Bulgari cocktail rings surged, the *Wall Street Journal* reported in 2004, as did yachts, custom-made boats, and Moët champagne.

The longer-term impact was more important. Bush's tax cuts meant that over the following decade vastly more money was in private hands, and correspondingly less was at the disposal of the federal government. The impact can be seen from the perspective of a single prominent family. Over the ten-year period from 2003 to 2012, the Bush tax cuts meant that the Walton family, owners of Wal-Mart, saved $3.9 billion in taxes they would have otherwise paid on dividends alone, with additional savings on capital gains and income taxes.

Overall, the Bush tax measures reduced income taxes in the United States to their lowest levels since World War II. At the same time, the cuts ushered in a new era of spiraling budget deficits, in which the federal government was forced to borrow more and more money to pay for its operations. In fiscal year 2000, just before Bush took office, the government ran a surplus of $86 billion. By the fiscal year ending in September 2008, just before the onset of the financial crisis, the government's deficit was $642 billion.

• • •

When he moved into the Oval Office, Bush decorated it with a series of paintings with Texas themes, including one of the Alamo, a reminder to visitors that his own self-image was different from that of his father. He walked with a jaunty bounce or swagger. At press conferences and in other public appearances, he sought to convey a sense of toughness. He spoke in an idiom that was part frontier Texas and part modern business executive.

Some of Bush's early initiatives moved American domestic policy decidedly to the right, pleasing the conservative constituencies that had supported his presidential campaign. He reversed several Clinton administration policies on environmental and social issues. Within two months after taking office, over the vehement objections of Christine Todd Whitman, whom he had appointed to run the Environmental Protection Agency, Bush reversed his own campaign pledge to regulate the emission of carbon dioxide by America's power plants. In the process, he rejected the goals of the Kyoto Protocol on greenhouse gas emissions. In announcing his decision, Bush cited what he called "the incomplete state of scientific knowledge of the causes of, and solutions to, global climate change," a statement that provided a stamp of presidential approval for years of challenges to scientists' warning about greenhouse gases.

Two days after taking office, Bush revived the so-called Mexico City policy on family planning, which required the U.S. Agency for International Development to deny funds to any organization, such as the Planned Parenthood Foundation, that supports abortion or provides counseling and information about it. The Mexico City policy had been adopted by the Reagan administration and rescinded by Clinton. (After Barack Obama succeeded Bush, he voided the policy once again.)

Bush also created a new Office of Faith-Based and Community Initiatives inside the White House, providing a way for religious and spiritual groups to obtain support and federal funds for social services. Its first director, University of Pennsylvania professor John DiIulio, departed within eight months in a storm of controversy, asserting that Bush's White House advisers paid more attention to the politics than to the substance of policy. Some Democrats charged that the program breached the separation of church and state; yet the program survived.

Modern American presidents have a tendency, in their first year or two on the job, to pick a single issue and study it for months before taking action, consulting numerous experts and exhaustively examining every possible aspect to the question. The hope seems to be that amid the torrent of other decisions, there will be at least one instance in which a new president can satisfy himself that he has taken the time to get all the information he possibly can. For Bill Clinton, that issue was health care, and for Barack Obama it was the war in Afghanistan. For George W. Bush, it was stem-cell research.

Two weeks after he was sworn in, Bush's domestic policy advisers informed him that legal guidelines issued by the Clinton administration had cleared the way for new federal funding of research using embryonic stem cells and that it would be up to Bush to decide whether to go forward. Bush viewed this question as one that pitted the interests of scientific research against the concerns raised by religious and right-to-life groups. He conducted what amounted to a prolonged seminar on the various aspects of stem-cell research.

Outside groups conducted intense lobbying campaigns for and against stem-cell research, so much so that Bush assigned Karl Rove as one of three staff aides to help him make a decision. Antiabortion and evangelical religious groups, a core element of Bush's electoral base, pointed out that stem-cell research was conducted with destroyed human embryos and that these embryos represented a form of life, in the same way as an aborted fetus.

On the other side of the issue, those favoring open-ended funding for stem-cell research included scientific researchers at the National Institutes of Health and many other organizations and individuals devoted to finding cures for various diseases, such as juvenile diabetes, Alzheimer's disease, and Parkinson's disease. One of the most prominent proponents was Nancy Reagan, whose husband, the former president, suffered from Alzheimer's disease; she wrote to Bush to urge that he support the "miracle possibilities" of stem-cell research.

Bush spent more than six months on the stem-cell decision before announcing his decision and then did so in the unusual form of an evening television address on August 9, 2001. In the end, he fashioned what he thought was a compromise. He banned federal funding for research from new stem-cell lines but carved out an exception under which the government would pay for continuing research on a small number of lines of stem cells that had previously been obtained, through private financing, from destroyed embryos. Scientific groups were embittered by his decision, while some religious and right-to-life groups attacked Bush for allowing a limited amount of research to proceed.

· · ·

On a single domestic issue, education, Bush followed the formula that he had used with considerable success as governor of Texas: find the most important Democratic legislative leader, work out an early compromise, and get a bill enacted with bipartisan support. The result was the program called No Child Left Behind, which would come to have an impact on a generation of schoolchildren across the country.

Bush had been setting forth his ideas for this program (including the name) since the earliest stages of his presidential campaign. He proposed a new requirement that each state set a series of uniform standards for basic skills, such as reading and math, and then administer a series of annual tests to students from third to eighth grade to evaluate how they were doing. The federal government would then provide support for students who lagged on these tests. The test results were also to be made public, school by school, with breakdowns of how various groups such as racial minorities or children from low-income families were performing. The aim, Bush explained, was to make schools and teachers more accountable by enabling parents to see for the first time how one school compared to others; if a school performed poorly, parents would be able to transfer their children elsewhere.

Bush introduced the legislation for No Child Left Behind during his first week in the White House. He immediately began to cultivate the most important Democratic legislator: Ted Kennedy, the ranking Democrat on the Senate committee responsible for education (and, also, unofficially, the most influential of all liberal Democrats). Bush invited Kennedy to a White House showing of *Thirteen Days*, a movie about the Cuban missile crisis, in which Kennedy's two older brothers had played the leading roles. He told Kennedy, "Let's show them Washington can still get things done." Kennedy made clear he was willing to work with Bush, sending him a note the following morning that said, "I look forward to some important White House signings."

Kennedy's interest lay in obtaining more attention and federal funding for the education of children in impoverished public schools. He also had a more generalized interest in winning Bush's support for the principle of a strong role for the federal government in education. He and other Democrats were strongly opposed, however, to a provision in Bush's legislation that would have enabled parents of children in failing schools to use vouchers, paid for by the federal government, to attend private schools.

Within four months after Bush took office, a compromise was reached. Bush dropped the proposal for private-school vouchers, in the process angering conservative educational leaders such as Reagan's secretary of education, William Bennett. In turn, Kennedy endorsed Bush's central idea of nationwide testing and standards, to the dismay of teachers' unions. The unions argued that poor student performance was usually the result of underlying social problems, not educational ones, and that No Child Left Behind would thus result in blaming schools and teachers unfairly.

When the bill was signed, Bush and Kennedy stood side by side at Boston Latin School, America's oldest public school, praising each other for their roles. Kennedy said that Bush had been "there every step of the way, making the difference on this legislation." Bush told Kennedy, "Not only are you a good senator, you are a good man."

With No Child Left Behind, Bush and Kennedy gave impetus to a broader movement for change in the nation's public schools. The legislation encouraged further state and local efforts to test students regularly and to use the results to evaluate the performance of schools and teachers. However, No Child Left Behind left a decidedly mixed legacy. Critics argued that it led to an obsession with standardized testing, creating pressure for schools and teachers to devote an inordinate time preparing children for the tests. In several cities, there were cheating scandals. A few years after the program was launched, Kennedy expressed disappointment with No Child Left Behind, claiming that the Bush administration had never provided the funds that he expected and that the program had been mismanaged. Worst of all, the law established standards so rigorous that large numbers of schools across the nation qualified as low performing, thus reducing the usefulness of the rating system. Eventually, the Obama administration granted a series of waivers that freed up most states from the strict requirements of No Child Left Behind.

· · ·

By the end of his first summer in the White House, Bush seemed to be putting himself in position to be remembered as a president devoted to two signature domestic issues: cutting taxes and reforming education. He frequently took part in public events meant to demonstrate the importance of education, and he had come to refer to himself as "the education president."

On the morning of September 11, 2001, Bush was at the Emma E. Booker Elementary School in Sarasota, Florida, preparing to watch second-grade students in a reading lesson, when airplanes struck the two World Trade Center towers, instantaneously redefining the nature of Bush's presidency.

4

———

September 11

When George W. Bush first came to the White House, most people expected that his foreign policy would be similar to his father's. During his campaign, he had surrounded himself with members of the George H. W. Bush administration. When questioned about his own lack of foreign-policy credentials, he would reply, "I've got one of the finest foreign policy teams ever assembled."

He filled out the top ranks of the administration with his father's senior aides: Vice President Dick Cheney had been his father's secretary of defense; Secretary of State Colin Powell had been chairman of the Joint Chiefs of Staff; Condoleezza Rice, the national security adviser, had served on the National Security Council staff for the elder Bush; Paul Wolfowitz and Richard Armitage, the deputy secretaries of defense and state, respectively, had also served in his father's administration. Commentators portrayed the new team as representing continuity with the past. Thomas L. Friedman of the *New York Times* used the word "retreads" to refer to the new Bush team. His fellow *Times* columnist Maureen Dowd agreed. "George II was an obedient son who emulated his father, the old king, in all respects. He felt no need to put his own stamp on his monarchy," wrote Dowd (a perception that ran contrary to her columns, years later, about the supposedly oedipal relationship between the two Bushes).

The columnists' misperceptions were understandable. It seems likely that at the beginning of the administration, neither George

W. Bush nor even his father understood the extent of the disagreements, rivalries, and conflicting worldviews among these officials.
George W. Bush had served as an occasional informal adviser in
his father's White House but only for politics and domestic policy,
and he knew few of the details of either the foreign policy of that
period or the personnel involved.

The most important dynamic was the unrecognized mistrust and
tension between Cheney and Powell. The two men had been partners running the Pentagon during the successful wars in Panama
and the Persian Gulf, but beneath the surface there had been a series
of conflicts. Powell had been the beneficiary of the 1986 Goldwater-
Nichols Act, which increased the authority of the chairman of the
Joint Chiefs of Staff; he became the most powerful occupant of that
job in history. Cheney and the civilians working under him at the
Pentagon had chafed at Powell's power, his role as a media star, and
the challenge they perceived to the principle of civilian control of
the military. Powell, in turn, regarded Cheney as too conservative
and too remote from the lives of ordinary soldiers, because he had
not served in the military. At one point during the George H. W.
Bush administration, Powell had kidded Cheney that his civilian
aides were "all right-wing nuts, like you."

George W. Bush's other appointments merely added to the internal discord. As secretary of defense, he nominated Donald Rumsfeld, who had served in the same job a quarter century earlier, during
the Ford administration. In fact, Rumsfeld had been Cheney's own
boss and mentor in the 1970s, and he proceeded to align himself
regularly with Cheney against Powell. Rumsfeld also developed an
antipathy toward Rice, complaining that she lacked sufficient experience or stature and that she too often infringed on his authority.
In turn, Rice thought that Rumsfeld had trouble treating her as an
equal.

It took remarkably little time for these submerged tensions to
burst forth. Less than two months after Bush's inauguration, President Kim Dae Jung of South Korea visited Washington. Just before
he arrived, the new Bush team decided to tell him that the administration planned to craft a new approach toward North Korea.

Early on the morning the meeting was to be held, however, Bush picked up the *Washington Post* and read a quote from Powell saying that in its North Korea policy, the new administration would pick up where the Clinton administration had left off. Furious, Bush woke up Rice and demanded she tell the new secretary of state to correct the record. Powell walked out of the meetings as they were taking place to tell reporters that the administration was reexamining in full the U.S. policy toward North Korea. Weeks later, he explained the incident away: "Sometimes, you get a little too far forward on your skis, that's all."

The following week, a decision by the new administration on greenhouse gas emissions pointed to another problem: some within the foreign-policy team were more attuned than others to America's allies overseas. Bush treated the decision not to curb carbon-dioxide emissions as primarily a matter of domestic policy involving the Environmental Protection Agency and Congress. He and Cheney sent a letter to Congress setting out the new policy and, in the process, denounced the Kyoto Protocol on climate change. When Rice saw the letter, she realized that it would infuriate European leaders; she alerted Powell, and they hurriedly sought to add a conciliatory sentence saying the Bush administration would continue to work with European governments to combat climate change. Bush rebuffed their pleas, claiming it was too late. A few weeks later, Bush attended a dinner with European leaders in Sweden at which, one after another, they attacked his policies on climate change. Bush didn't take this criticism well. "The President was really angry, and he never fully forgave what he saw as the disrespectful tone taken at the dinner," reported Rice. The Kyoto announcement, Rice later acknowledged, helped to crystallize the European view that Bush took a unilateral approach to foreign policy.

Other actions by Bush in his early months further contributed to this perception of unilateralism. The Bush administration sought to undercut or reject several international treaties and agreements, in the process upsetting its allies overseas, especially those in Europe. Bush turned down an international protocol to enforce bans on biological weapons and asked for changes in an international agreement on the sale of small arms. In its final year, the outgoing Clinton administration had taken steps toward joining the International Criminal Court; Bush quickly reversed course.

Bush had promised during the campaign to withdraw from the 1972 Anti-Ballistic Missile Treaty, which stood as an impediment to the construction of missile-defense systems. In the new administration's early months, scuttling the ABM treaty became the top item on the agenda for Bush's foreign policy. His advisers, particularly Cheney and Rumsfeld, contended that new missile-defense systems were necessary to shield the United States against missiles from countries such as North Korea and Iran. "We had to be able to build systems that could intercept incoming missiles if we were to keep the country safe, but the ABM Treaty wouldn't permit us to do it," argued Cheney.

Those words captured both the spirit of Bush's approach to foreign policy during his early months in office and its underlying defect. The new president and his more experienced advisers were trying to adapt America's national security policies for the post–cold war world. In doing so, however, they were focused almost entirely on threats from other nation-states, such as Iran, North Korea, Iraq, China, or Russia.

Bush and his advisers devoted considerably less attention in those early months to the potential threats from nonstate actors, that is, from organizations existing outside the boundaries or territory of a single country, notably the murky group called al-Qaeda. Its attacks on the United States had begun with the World Trade Center bombing in February 1993, a month after the George H. W. Bush administration left office. During Clinton's presidency, al-Qaeda had become a growing preoccupation, as it carried out lethal attacks against the American embassies in Kenya and Tanzania in 1998, killing hundreds of people, and against the USS *Cole* at a port in Yemen in 2000, killing seventeen American sailors. Several other al-Qaeda plots had been foiled, including one at the turn of the new millennium.

The result was a paradox: in 2001, Bush thought of his foreign-policy team as a group of old, experienced hands, but in one important aspect of national security policy, dealing with al-Qaeda, they had little experience at all. During the presidential transition, Clinton officials tried to warn Bush and his aides about the threat of terrorist attacks, but the message didn't take hold. Bill Clinton later testified to the 9/11 Commission that before leaving office he had told Bush, "I think that you will find that by far your biggest threat is Bin Laden and the al-Qaeda." Bush told the commission, however, that he didn't remember being told much about al-Qaeda. Samuel D. Berger, Clinton's outgoing national security adviser, said he delivered a similar warning to Rice, but she claimed that he spent most of the meeting talking about the Middle East peace process and North Korea. Rice kept Richard Clarke, the National Security Council's counterterrorism specialist, on the job, and he quickly called for stepped-up efforts by the new administration against al-Qaeda, but she was wary of him.

The new administration's approach to terrorism in the early months of 2001 was best summarized by George Tenet, who served as CIA director under Clinton and Bush and was generally on good terms with both presidents. "At the top tier, there was a loss of urgency," Tenet later wrote. "Unless you have experienced terrorism on your watch—unless you have been on the receiving end of a 4:00 A.M. phone call telling you that one of your embassies or one of your ships has just been attacked, it is hard to fathom the impact of such a loss."

In May, Tenet warned Bush that U.S. intelligence was picking up growing "chatter" about a new attack by al-Qaeda. Much of the intelligence seemed to point to an attack overseas, similar to the earlier ones in Africa and Yemen. In response, security was tightened at several U.S. embassies. On several occasions, Bush asked CIA officials to examine whether there might be an attack on the American homeland. They responded with a briefing memo that was published in the President's Daily Brief on August 6, 2001, under the headline "Bin Laden Determined to Strike in U.S." Bush later maintained that this memo was of limited utility because it contained mostly historical material and lacked concrete information about how or when a new attack would be carried out.

Both the CIA and the FBI missed a series of clues to what was coming. Al-Qaeda had sent a series of operatives from abroad to the United States, and in the summer of 2001 some of them signed up for instruction in how to fly airplanes. The Bush administration, meanwhile, was moving very slowly. Its first top-level meeting to discuss a strategy for al-Qaeda was held in early September. The officials decided to launch unmanned Predator drones for reconnaissance over Afghanistan, and on September 10 Rice forwarded the decision to Bush for his approval.

It was too late. Early the following morning, al-Qaeda operatives commandeered four commercial planes and steered three of them into the two World Trade Center towers and the Pentagon.

• • •

During the cold war, the U.S. government had carried out an extensive series of drills to plan what to do in case of a nuclear attack on the United States. These were called continuity-of-government exercises; they were aimed at ensuring that all of America's top leaders would not be killed at the same time and that communications between civilian leaders and the military could not be disrupted. Cheney had taken part in these exercises and was far more familiar with them than Bush was. It was no surprise, then, that in the hours after the September 11 attacks, Cheney took charge of the administration's decision making, operating primarily from the bunker under the White House.

On this day that would define his presidency and change the course of history, Bush unhappily found himself at the education event in Sarasota. It was Cheney who gave the tense order, amid fear of continuing attacks, to shoot down any commercial plane believed to have been hijacked. He and Bush would later claim that the vice president cleared this decision with the president over the phone beforehand, but there is no record of such a conversation and reason to doubt it ever took place.

Bush said he wanted to come back to the White House, but his aides ordered him not to do so, because they thought Washington was unsafe and because the president and vice president should not be in the same location. "I then did something that I never did again," Rice subsequently wrote. "I raised my voice with the president and in a tone as firm as I could possibly muster, I said, 'Mr. President, you cannot come back here. Washington, I mean the United States, is under attack.'" Over the course of the day, Bush was flown first to Barksdale Air Force Base in Louisiana (where he appeared in a grainy, unpolished video that his own aides admitted was far from reassuring) and then, for better communications, to the Strategic Command in Nebraska. Finally, saying that he needed to be able to speak to the nation from the White House, Bush insisted to the Secret Service that he needed to return to Washington. He landed there in the early evening, while Cheney flew off to Camp David. Bush gave a brief television address to the nation that night. "Today, our nation saw evil," he said. "The search is under way for those who are behind these evil acts."

Over the following days, Bush took on the role of a wartime president. He presided over a national prayer service at the National Cathedral, with his father and former presidents Ford, Carter, and Clinton in attendance. He visited Washington's Islamic Center, where he urged the public to avoid discrimination or hate crimes against Arabs or Muslims. He went to Ground Zero, amid the rubble of the fallen World Trade Center towers. Rescue workers greeted him with chants of "U.S.A., U.S.A." Through a bullhorn, he shouted to them, "The rest of the world hears you, and the people who knocked these buildings down will hear all of us soon!" In a speech to a joint session of Congress, he prepared the nation for military action, declaring that the campaign he planned would not relent "until every terrorist group of global reach has been found, stopped and defeated."

In those days of crisis, he sometimes fell back on his self-image as a tough-talking Texan. Referring to bin Laden, he quipped, "There's an old poster out West, I recall, that says, 'Wanted, Dead or Alive.'" Several of his aides warned that he shouldn't personalize America's response to September 11 in this way. Years later, Bush himself would reflect that those words were "a little too blunt."

The public response at the time, however, was overwhelmingly positive. Just before September 11, the Gallup Poll had reported that Bush's approval rating stood at 51 percent, meaning that, just as at the time of the 2000 presidential election, the nation was almost evenly divided. Ten days after the attacks, Gallup and other polls reported that the figure had jumped to 90 percent, a level as high as that for his father at the end of the Persian Gulf War and higher than that for any other president.

The press coverage was similarly enthusiastic. After the prayer service and the visit to Ground Zero, R. W. Apple Jr. wrote in the *New York Times* that Bush "began coming of age this weekend" and that "he made significant progress toward easing the doubts about his capacity for the job and the legitimacy of his election." After the speech to Congress, the *Times* editorialized that "he was as strong and forthright as the nation could have wished." The Democrats joined in the praise. "He's done a first-rate job," said Joseph R. Biden Jr., the chairman of the Senate Foreign Relations Committee. "Count me in on the 90 percent [who approve]."

Amid this outpouring of support, however, Bush and his aides were quietly making fundamental policy choices and embracing themes that attracted far less attention but would set the stage for future acrimony.

The first was the notion of an unlimited war on terror and, along with it, a continuing emphasis on the role of nation-states and their leaders. Bush's first speech to the nation on the night of September 11 contained a vaguely worded warning to other governments. "We will make no distinction between the terrorists who committed these acts and those who harbor them," the president declared. This was not merely a speechwriter's turn of phrase; Bush and Rice had parsed these words and had cleared them with Cheney, Rumsfeld, and Powell. This language was undefined; Rice said it reflected simply a belief that since terrorist groups have no territory or sovereignty to lose, it is easier to issue a warning to a state.

But to which countries did Bush's wording apply? Everyone agreed it meant Afghanistan, whose Taliban regime had allowed bin Laden and other al-Qaeda leaders to take up residence, carry out operations, and run terrorist training camps for the previous five years. What about Pakistan, which was both a close friend of the United States and also the main patron of the Taliban? What about countries in the Middle East or the Persian Gulf?

Early on the morning of September 12, less than twenty-four hours after the attacks, Tenet showed up at the White House to give the president his daily intelligence briefing. Just outside the West Wing, he ran into Richard Perle, officially the head of the advisory Defense Policy Board and unofficially a leader of the neoconservative movement that had espoused a hawkish American foreign policy both in the cold war and in its aftermath. "Iraq has to pay a price for what happened yesterday. They bear responsibility," Perle told the CIA director. That weekend, when Bush summoned his top foreign-policy officials to Camp David to decide on military responses to the September 11 attacks, Paul Wolfowitz, the deputy secretary of defense and another leading neoconservative, argued specifically for military action against Iraq, arguing that it was of greater strategic importance to the United States than Afghanistan.

They and other hawks, both inside and outside the Bush administration, argued that the United States needed to go further than simply retaliating against al-Qaeda. They pointed out that previous efforts at retaliation against al-Qaeda—notably, President Clinton's decision to fire cruise missiles at training camps in Afghanistan after the embassy bombings of 1998—had been ineffective at stopping terrorist attacks.

Bush and Rice agreed with this point of view. "Dropping expensive weapons on sparsely populated camps would not break the Taliban's hold on the country or destroy al-Qaeda's sanctuary," Bush explained in his memoir. At the time, he put this thought more pithily: he said he wanted to do more than "pound sand."

The second development of significance lay in the decision by Bush and most of his senior advisers that America's response to September 11 would be essentially unilateral in nature. On the day after the attacks, the leaders of the North Atlantic Treaty Organization did something they had never done before: they approved a resolution under Article V of the North Atlantic Treaty, the provision of collective self-defense in which an armed attack on any member of the treaty is considered an attack on all of them. This action reflected the wave of sympathy for the United States in Europe; on September 12, the French newspaper *Le Monde* had declared on its front page: "We Are All Americans."

Bush, however, kept the Europeans at arm's length. He and other administration officials were reluctant to coordinate America's response to September 11 too closely with other countries. Military leaders recalled how time-consuming and cumbersome it had been to reach decisions within NATO for military actions in Bosnia and Kosovo in the 1990s. Moreover, America had now been hit on its own soil. Explaining the administration's aloofness toward NATO at the time, Rice wrote ruefully a decade later, "We were single-minded, bruised, and determined to avenge 9/11 as quickly as possible. Nonetheless, I've always felt that we left the Alliance dressed up with nowhere to go."

Instead of collective action, Bush and his team came up with a different concept: they would act together with shifting, ad hoc coalitions of countries. "The mission must determine the coalition. The coalition ought not determine the mission," Rumsfeld told Bush in a memo. This left it to the United States to decide which actions to take. Rumsfeld said he got the idea from a conversation with Benjamin Netanyahu, the former Israeli prime minister, then out of office, who warned him that acting through any formal alliance would restrict America's flexibility. Thus was born the notion of a "coalition of the willing," a central concept for Bush and his team as they began to move toward a military response to the September 11 attacks.

At the meeting with his war cabinet at Camp David the weekend after September 11, Bush was presented with three different military options: to strike al-Qaeda camps in Afghanistan with cruise missiles, as Clinton had done; to attack with both missiles and bombers, hitting a wider range of targets; or, finally, to mount a full invasion with American troops to dislodge the Taliban. Bush chose the third option. "This time, we would put boots on the ground, and keep them there until the Taliban and al-Qaeda were driven out and a free society could emerge," he concluded.

At the same time, Bush rejected Wolfowitz's proposal for immediate military action against Iraq. Powell had argued strenuously against moving on Iraq on grounds that it would fracture the international support that had been forming for action against the Taliban. Tenet was also strongly opposed, on grounds that the administration ought to focus on al-Qaeda. Both Cheney and Rice agreed that, for the time being, acting against Iraq would be a distraction.

Bush agreed, and the question of attacking Iraq was set aside, not rejected but deferred. The administration would first concentrate on Afghanistan, he decided. He announced the plans in his speech to Congress. In doing so, he set forth another theme that would become a hallmark of the early Bush years. "Every nation, in every region, now has a decision to make," Bush said. "Either you are with us, or you are with the terrorists."

. . .

Soon after September 11, Bush began to approve a far-reaching set of changes on the home front. His actions would come to affect everything from daily life and travel throughout the United States to the operations of the federal government, the legal authority of the presidency, and the powers of America's intelligence and national security agencies. Some of Bush's actions were adopted openly; others were made on "the dark side," in the phrase made famous by Cheney.

Almost instantly, American air travel was transformed. All air traffic had come to a halt on the morning of September 11. When it resumed, travelers were subject to the extensive searches that became a permanent feature of air travel. For a time, National Guard units were assigned to airports, and air marshals were placed on many commercial flights. Bush quickly appointed Tom Ridge, the governor of Pennsylvania, to a new post, initially as the White House official in charge of homeland security and eventually as the secretary of a new cabinet agency, the Department of Homeland

Security. DHS took charge of immigration, customs, border patrol, and the newly created Transportation Security Agency.

Bush went to Congress for legislation that would strengthen the authority of the Justice Department and the FBI. Within six weeks, Congress approved the bill, which was called the USA Patriot Act, a name that came from Congress and that Bush later claimed he regretted for its implication that its opponents were unpatriotic. "I should have pushed Congress to change the name of the bill before I signed it," he wrote after leaving office. The law removed the wall of separation between intelligence collection and law enforcement, permitting extensive new sharing of information. It authorized new kinds of roving wiretaps. It also opened the way for the government to examine credit card bills, leases, and even the library records of those suspected of terrorist activity; the last provision, which became a rallying cry for privacy experts, was unpopular even with Laura Bush, a former librarian.

The first actions on "the dark side" also began within weeks after September 11. Bush had been surprised to discover that al-Qaeda not only had infiltrated its agents into the United States without detection but also had communicated with them from Afghanistan. His and his aides' anxieties were further compounded by the anthrax scare, in which letters with anthrax spores were sent to various news media outlets and to members of Congress. The Bush team worried that a second attack might be coming soon, perhaps from additional "sleeper cells" of al-Qaeda agents in the United States.

Bush's response was to authorize the highly classified program in which the National Security Agency conducted electronic surveillance of communications into and out of the United States without a warrant. This measure, later called the Terrorist Surveillance Program, would eventually spawn more than a decade of controversy, at first inside the Bush administration and then with the public under both Bush and Barack Obama. The extensive NSA surveillance activities made public by Edward J. Snowden in 2013 are an updated version of the program Bush approved the month after the September 11 attacks.

This surveillance program had two characteristics that would set the pattern for other Bush actions on the "dark side." One was that Bush's primary role was not as initiator, but to give his imprimatur to actions drawn up by those working under him, especially Cheney. The vice president was the driving force on the surveillance program, at first asking intelligence officials what new authority they needed to broaden the scope of their monitoring of al-Qaeda and then meeting with Michael Hayden, the NSA director, and with Tenet to work out the details of the new program.

The other characteristic, paradoxically, is that although Bush had a minimal role in devising the secretive programs, his approval of them served to expand the power of the presidency. The Foreign Intelligence Surveillance Act of 1978 required U.S. officials to go to a secret court for a warrant before spying on foreign agents inside the United States, which meant that Bush needed some explanation for why the NSA did not have to obtain a warrant from the secret court to approve its expanded surveillance. Cheney worked with his aide David Addington, White House counsel Alberto Gonzales, and John Yoo of the Justice Department to come up with legal justification. Their analysis relied mainly on the fact that the nation was at war and that American presidents, including Abraham Lincoln and Franklin Roosevelt, had historically assumed additional constitutional powers in wartime. Furthermore, in the week after September 11, Congress had passed a resolution, called the Authorization for the Use of Military Force, with expansive language that the government lawyers maintained could justify the NSA surveillance. Bush signed the order for the new NSA program on October 4, requiring that the program be reauthorized every forty-five days. For nearly three years, those authorizations were routine.

Two days later, Bush ordered the start of military action in Afghanistan, with the aim of overthrowing the Taliban regime. Here Bush played an entirely different role: he was not merely the ratifier of his subordinates' decisions but the initiator: an impatient, hands-on president who pressed and cajoled those under him to move in the direction he wanted. When the Pentagon moved slowly to develop a war plan for Afghanistan, Bush called Rice out of an afternoon meeting at the CIA and demanded: "I want a plan tomorrow. Call Don [Rumsfeld], and make sure I have one." Weeks later, when the war started and America's Afghan allies the Northern Alliance hesitated to engage the Taliban, Bush was similarly impatient. "They just need to move," he said.

There were a few days in late October when the war seemed to bog down, and commentators began to worry about a "quagmire." But this turned out to be a short military campaign that seemed, at the time, to end in an overwhelming victory. The Taliban fled from Kabul on November 15 and from its last stronghold in Kandahar on December 7. Fifteen days later, with strong support from the United States, Hamid Karzai was inaugurated as president of a new Afghan government. However, the sense of triumph was incomplete: Osama bin Laden had fled into the mountainous caves of Tora Bora and escaped.

• • •

The end of the Afghanistan campaign opened a new set of issues for Bush and resulted in a flurry of new actions, many of them made in secret, that would prove at least as controversial as the NSA surveillance. In the course of the war, American forces and their Afghan allies began to capture many Taliban and al-Qaeda prisoners. The Bush administration needed to decide where to put them and what rules should govern their detention.

Bush, together with Cheney, made the first decision just before the fall of Kabul: those who were taken captive could be held indefinitely and then subjected to special military tribunals similar to those set up by Franklin Roosevelt for Nazi saboteurs in World War II. The detainees would not be tried in U.S. courts or by any international body. Within the U.S. government, an interagency group headed by a State Department official had been assigned to resolve the complex legal issues surrounding detention, but before it could finish its work it was preempted. Addington, Cheney's legal adviser, drafted an order setting up the new system of tribunals; Cheney took it to Bush over lunch, and Bush signed it later that day. Some of Bush's top aides, including Rice and Attorney General John Ash-croft, objected to this hurried and secretive process but to no avail.

Next, the administration needed a place to hold those whom it captured. Tommy Franks, the U.S. military commander in charge of the war, made clear that he did not want to keep prisoners inside Afghanistan. The issue took on heightened urgency after the first American death in the war: CIA operative Johnny Spann was killed in a riot in an Afghan jail where he had gone to interrogate those detained there. For reasons of security, bringing prisoners back to the United States was out of the question. But if not in Afghanistan or the United States, where would the prisoners go?

Cheney again took the lead. "The Vice President was, as I remember it, the one who suggested that we find an 'offshore' facility," recalled Rice. A solution was soon found: detainees were taken to Guantánamo Bay, the U.S. naval base on the southern coast of Cuba. Guantánamo was isolated, making it impossible for prisoners to escape. Bush believed that Guantánamo offered a unique benefit that set it apart from U.S. bases in other remote locations or islands his aides had briefly considered, such as Guam. Because of its unusual legal status (the United States operates Guantánamo under a long-term lease dating back to the Spanish-American War), it is not considered American territory. As a result, the detainees held at Guantánamo would have no access to the U.S. court system and no constitutional protections, such as the right to remain silent.

The next question to be decided was whether the detainees were entitled to the protections of the Geneva Conventions, which require humane treatment of prisoners of war. In early 2002, this issue engendered intense disagreement among Bush's advisers. A proposal drafted by Justice Department lawyers held that the Geneva Conventions didn't apply to any of the detainees; it argued that al-Qaeda was a stateless entity with no rights at all under international law and that Afghanistan was a failed state whose Taliban regime was recognized by only a handful of governments, so that Taliban prisoners had no rights, either.

The ensuing debate produced the first signs of tension among Bush's advisers between those who had served in the military and those who had not, causing divisions that would reemerge, with considerably more acrimony, in the debate over Iraq. Military leaders have long been schooled in the importance of the Geneva Conventions, not merely for their own sake but for the protection they provide to captured American soldiers. General Richard Myers, the chairman of the Joint Chiefs of Staff, was so incensed that the U.S. government was trying to "weasel out" of applying the Geneva Conventions that he stormed into Rumsfeld's office to object.

Bush initially decided that the Geneva Conventions simply didn't apply. Then Powell, himself a former chairman of the Joint Chiefs, weighed in, arguing strenuously that the Geneva Conventions should cover all the detainees. By early 2002, pictures of hooded prisoners arriving at Guantánamo were appearing around the world, and the secretary of state was beginning to get protests from America's European allies about improper treatment.

Powell asked for a National Security Council meeting to examine the issue. Bush was annoyed, because he thought he had already made his decision, but he held the session anyway. After a few days, in a nod to Powell, he modified his earlier decision slightly, deciding that while the Geneva Conventions did not apply to al-Qaeda, they did apply at least in theory to the war in Afghanistan and thus to soldiers of the Taliban regime. But the Taliban detainees were still held to be unlawful combatants, not prisoners of war who would be entitled to the full protections of Geneva. In a written memo, Bush promised that as a matter of policy the U.S. armed forces would continue to treat detainees "humanely" and in a way consistent with the Geneva Conventions, "to the extent appropriate and consistent with military necessity," qualifications that limited the extent of protection under the conventions. (Later on, the Supreme Court would decide that the detainees were entitled to greater protection under the Geneva Conventions than Bush had given them.)

Bush's decision applied to treatment of prisoners by the armed forces but not by the CIA. There was a reason for this distinction, not obvious at the time. A handful of captured al-Qaeda members were not sent to Guantánamo. Instead, the CIA set up its own covert prison system around the world where it brought the most important al-Qaeda leaders for interrogation. These so-called black sites were eventually located in at least eight countries, including Poland, Romania, Thailand, and Afghanistan itself.

The rules for interrogation had been an underlying issue during the legal debate on the Geneva Conventions, which stipulate that prisoners of war cannot be punished for refusing to cooperate. Gonzales and Addington had argued in a memo to Bush that the war on terrorism was a different kind of war and that "this paradigm renders obsolete Geneva's strict limitation on questioning of enemy prisoners."

Within weeks after resolving the legal debate over detainees, Bush was confronted with the far more concrete related questions: How far could the CIA go in interrogating prisoners? What could it do to make someone talk? On March 28, 2002, Tenet called the president excitedly to report that the CIA had taken control of its first high-level al-Qaeda operative, Abu Zubaydeh, who had been captured in Pakistan with help from the Pakistani police. After answering some initial questions, Zubaydeh stopped talking, but his CIA handlers felt he was holding back on additional, useful information.

Thus began what eventually became known as the CIA's "enhanced interrogation program." Tenet sought approval to use a variety of techniques to get the CIA's detainees to talk and to cooperate with their interrogators. Bush asked the Justice Department whether the program would be violating any laws and was told that the harsh techniques would be legal, the justification coming in a series of written opinions that were later dubbed the "torture memos." Justice Department officials turned down only one of the CIA's proposed techniques: to bury a prisoner alive until he believed he was suffocating. Bush said he also turned down two of the CIA's proposals. But Bush approved the other techniques, such as slapping, sleep deprivation, loud noises, and the most controversial of all, "waterboarding," in which water is poured over a prisoner's face until he feels he is drowning.

Using these methods, CIA investigators got Abu Zubaydeh to provide information that helped lead to the capture a year later of Khalid Sheikh Mohammed, the senior al-Qaeda official in charge of the September 11 operations and, later on, the beheading of Daniel Pearl, a *Wall Street Journal* reporter who had been kidnapped and killed in Pakistan. When Tenet asked for permission to use waterboarding on Khalid Sheikh Mohammed, Bush retorted, "Damn right." The al-Qaeda leader was subjected to waterboarding 183 times. Years later, Bush reflected, "Khalid Sheikh Mohammed proved difficult to break. But when he did, he gave us a lot." The remarks underscored Bush's close involvement with the interrogation program.

When the enhanced interrogation program became public several years later, many people in the United States (including, eventually, Bush's successor Barack Obama) maintained that waterboarding and the broader CIA program amounted to torture—and, indeed, they seemed to fit the dictionary definition of the word. Bush frequently responded to such accusations by saying, simply, "We don't torture," without offering further elaboration. He did not mention that there was a strong incentive to avoid using the word "torture": it is banned by a series of laws and international treaties. In his memoir, Bush pointed out that "the most senior legal officers in the U.S. government" had assured him the CIA program did not amount to torture. Beyond that, Bush argued that the enhanced interrogation was necessary to stop al-Qaeda from mounting another attack on the United States. "Had I not authorized waterboarding on senior al-Qaeda leaders, I would have had to accept a greater risk that the country would be attacked," he wrote.

· · ·

In sum, over the course of the first seven months after September 11, largely in secret, Bush authorized a sweeping series of responses to the attacks that transformed the operations of America's homeland security apparatus, its intelligence gathering and operations, and its approach to international law and treatment of prisoners. He had not only uprooted the Taliban regime in Afghanistan but also set up the legal and institutional framework for a prolonged "war on terror."

Robert Gates, who joined the Bush administration five years after most of these measures were adopted, later attributed them in part to what he called "the traumatic effect" of September 11 upon the entire Bush team. "I think there was a huge sense among senior members of the administration of having let the country down, of having allowed a devastating attack on America to take place on their watch," wrote Gates, saying he based this judgment on private conversations with senior administration officials. At the time, he noted, the administration was being deluged with reports of further, imminent attacks, including rumors that a nuclear weapon might be set off in New York or Washington. Getting more intelligence and preventing another attack became "the sole pre-occupation of the president and his senior team," Gates explained. "Any obstacle—legal, bureaucratic, financial, or international—to accomplishing those objectives had to be overcome."

5

Iraq

George W. Bush had made clear from the outset that the removal of the Taliban would be merely the start, not the end, of his government's response to September 11. "Our war on terrorism begins with al Qaeda but it does not end there," he had declared in his speech to Congress nine days after the attacks. Powell had said that Afghanistan represented merely "phase one" of a larger campaign.

The administration's statements suggested an obvious question: if Afghanistan was phase one of the war on terror, what would be phase two? Would there be another military campaign against another failed state in which al-Qaeda had taken root, such as Yemen, the Sudan, or the Philippines? In the weeks immediately after the fall of Kabul, U.S. intelligence for a time had placed Somalia under intense surveillance in what was seen at the time as a prelude to a possible military strike. Yet none of these other countries seemed important enough to qualify as a prime target for the next phase of a major war. None had regimes as malevolent as the Taliban. It would be difficult to sustain public attention and support for a second military action if it were waged against some marginal country whose defeat might be perceived as merely cumulative, or anticlimactic, after Afghanistan. Bush had now defined his entire presidency in terms of the "war on terror"; after Afghanistan, that war needed to be reoriented with goals that were far reaching but also concrete.

Over the course of the fall of 2001, the public statements about the war on terror by Bush and the senior officials of his administration began to change in subtle ways. At first, administration officials spoke primarily of the dangers of al-Qaeda and other terrorist organizations. Then they began to call attention to the danger that such terrorist groups might acquire nuclear, biological, or chemical weapons. After a bit more time, administration officials began to voice alarms about the possibility that governments could provide weapons of mass destruction to terrorist groups. Finally, they began to focus more narrowly on the handful of countries they considered dangerous. The veterans of the Bush team were thus recasting the war on terror in a familiar way, once again emphasizing the role of states rather than nonstate actors.

In his State of the Union speech on January 29, 2002, Bush served notice to the world of this profound change in approach. He announced that his administration was targeting countries that were seeking to acquire weapons of mass destruction and might be willing to provide them to terrorists. He named, specifically, three countries—Iran, Iraq, and North Korea—branding them as an "axis of evil," although he provided no evidence that the three of them were working together in the fashion of the Axis powers in World War II. The "axis of evil" rhetoric marked a watershed in Bush's foreign policy; it opened what became a chasm between the United States and its European allies as European leaders quickly denounced Bush and his speech.

Of the three regimes in the "axis of evil," two seemed impregnable. North Korea could respond to any military attack with a quick, massive artillery attack that would destroy Seoul. Iran, too, represented a daunting military challenge; moreover, it had strong commercial relationships with many of America's allies, including France, Germany, and Japan.

This recognition brought Bush back to Iraq. It was the lone member of the "axis" with which the United States already had an official policy in favor of regime change, signed into law by President Bill Clinton in the late 1990s. Foreign-policy hawks inside and outside the Bush administration had been urging a military attack on Iraq since the day after September 11, maintaining (without evidence) that Saddam Hussein's regime bore some responsibility for what al-Qaeda had perpetrated.

Bush had said no to attacking Iraq at the time, but he had said only that he was deferring a decision while the United States concentrated on Afghanistan. After the fall of the Taliban, as the administration considered the question of what would be the "second phase" of the war on terror, it did not take long before Bush reached the likely answer: Iraq.

In November 2001, the president asked Donald Rumsfeld to review the battle plans for Iraq, and before the end of the year General Tommy Franks, the commander of the U.S. Central Command, visited Bush to present the first in what would become a series of increasingly refined battle plans for an invasion of Iraq. In April 2002, Bush and his wife, Laura, welcomed British Prime Minister Tony Blair and his wife, Cherie, to the new ranch house the Bushes had just completed in Crawford, Texas. Bush and Blair agreed that it was time to do something about the Iraqi president, Saddam Hussein.

• • •

In the aftermath of September 11, Bush saw himself as following the model of one particular American president, Harry S. Truman. Bush was not the first chief executive to feel this way: Truman has regularly been a figure of consolation for presidents who believe that while they may be unpopular during their time in the White House, they will be admired decades later. Moreover, for Bush, Truman carried additional significance: he served as president as the United States was entering a new era, and the Truman administration established not merely the institutions but the foreign-policy strategy and doctrines for a different world.

Rice, Bush's closest adviser, had reinforced this line of thinking. As a former Soviet specialist, she was steeped in the history of the cold war and its origins. After September 11, she, too, found it easy to fit the tasks the Bush administration was confronting into the new-era paradigm of Truman's presidency. When Bush finished reading David McCullough's biography of Truman, Rice persuaded him to read former secretary of state Dean Acheson's memoir, *Present at the Creation*. Both Bush and Rice were convinced that after September 11 it was time to jettison old doctrines, to challenge existing assumptions, and to create new principles for dealing with the world.

As Bush began to turn his attention to Iraq, the idea of military action was constrained by the reigning ideas left over from the cold war. The United States had elected not to wage war with the Soviet Union but to wait it out; instead of military action, American leaders had developed the doctrines of containment and deterrence. Those ideas would have weighed against military action in Iraq, as long as Saddam Hussein did not go to war first. But Bush and Rice decided that, just as Truman and his team had established new doctrines for the cold war, the Bush administration should do similarly for its campaign against terrorism.

On June 1, 2002, delivering the commencement address at West Point, Bush served notice of this new approach. Americans should be ready for "preemptive action" to protect national security, he said, adding, "We must take the battle to the enemy, disrupt his plans and confront the worst threats before they emerge." He was effectively discarding containment and deterrence. Three months later, Rice enshrined this change in a document called the National Security Strategy of 2002. The United States "will not hesitate to act alone, if necessary, to exercise our right of self-defense by acting preemptively," declared this formal statement of the administration's strategy.

. . .

By the summer of 2002, as it became increasingly clear that Bush was laying the groundwork for war with Iraq, the simmering public debate reached a boil. The growing opposition came not merely from Democrats, peace groups, and isolationists but also from the top levels of the foreign-policy elite. In mid-August, the *Wall Street Journal*'s conservative op-ed page published a piece with the simple headline "Don't Attack Saddam." The article argued that attacking Iraq would not be the next step in the war on terror but rather a diversion from it; a military campaign against Saddam Hussein would undoubtedly be very expensive and could also be bloody.

The author was Brent Scowcroft, no ordinary dissenter. He had been the national security adviser to Bush's father and was the coauthor of the senior Bush's presidential memoir. He had also been a mentor to Condoleezza Rice. His article challenged head-on Bush's and Rice's arguments about the need for a new strategy in a new era. "Saddam is a familiar dictatorial aggressor, with traditional goals for his aggression," Scowcroft wrote.

Bush and Rice were angered. Bush called his father, who assured him, "Son, Brent is a friend." Scowcroft's piece prompted public speculation that it was actually a veiled message from George H. W. Bush to his son about war with Iraq. However, there has never been any evidence to support that speculation. Scowcroft was fully capable of speaking on his own, with only foreign policy in mind and not the Bush family. Indeed, George H. W. Bush never spoke out against the Iraq War. (Seven months later, just after George W. Bush ordered the start of military operations, his father wrote him a letter in which he said: "You are doing the right thing . . . You have done that which you had to do.")

Nevertheless, Scowcroft's op-ed did reflect the views of another old friend, Secretary of State Colin Powell. In early August 2002, in his longest conversation with Bush since the inauguration, Powell warned about the impact of war and the difficulties of rebuilding Iraq afterward. When Bush asked Powell how he would handle Iraq, the secretary of state replied, "Take it to the U.N." Scowcroft made the same argument in his article, opening the floodgates for other high-level opposition to immediate military action. Over the following days, former secretaries of state James Baker and Lawrence Eagleburger also issued public warnings against war with Iraq until the issue was brought before the U.N. Security Council.

Cheney spearheaded the other side of this debate, both inside the administration and in the public arena. In a speech to the Veterans of Foreign Wars, he argued that Saddam Hussein was already in violation of existing Security Council resolutions and that there was no need to go back to the U.N. Doing so, he argued, would only give the Iraqi leader the time and leeway to procrastinate. "Saddam has perfected the art of cheat and retreat, and is very skilled in the art of denial and deception," Cheney declared. Hearing this speech, Bush felt the vice president's rhetoric was boxing him in. He ordered Rice to call Cheney and tell him the president had not yet made up his mind. Cheney soon gave a softer speech, with language dictated by Rice.

Bush was now confronted with a decision on how to proceed: whether to move quickly toward war, as Cheney proposed, or to go the United Nations, as Powell, his father's advisers, and Tony Blair all strongly favored. In early September, he chose the latter option, on grounds that it would help to win support from the international community and to call attention to Saddam Hussein's continuing defiance of the United Nations. Then, if the Iraqi leader did not comply, there would be a stronger basis for war. When Blair agreed to support this approach, Bush told one of Blair's aides, "Your man has got *cojones.*"

Bush also decided to seek congressional authorization for the use of force. Throughout the fall of 2002, he and his aides sought to line up votes both in Congress and at the U.N. Security Council. In Congress, the question of timing was crucial: should the vote be held before or after the midterm elections in November? Senate Majority Leader Tom Daschle later said he scheduled the vote before the election only because Bush personally asked him to do so; Daschle said he was told that "time was of the essence." He and other Democrats believed that Karl Rove, Bush's political strategist, had favored a preelection vote to pressure Democrats to either support Bush or be accused of being weak on national security. Rove later said he had argued for a postelection vote in Congress because it would be perceived as uninfluenced by political considerations; he said Rice and other foreign-policy advisers did not want to wait, because a congressional resolution of support for Bush could be helpful at the Security Council.

In the 'end, Bush decided to go for a congressional vote in early
October, a month before the election. The Senate voted 77 to 23
and the House 296 to 133 to authorize the use of force against Iraq.
Leading Democrats, among them Senators John Kerry, Joe Biden,
Hillary Clinton, John Edwards, and Chris Dodd and House Minority Leader Dick Gephardt, voted in favor of the resolution. In the
final weeks of the midterm election campaigns, Republicans accused
Democratic candidates who had opposed the resolution of weakness or even a lack of patriotism. In Georgia, an attack ad against
Senator Max Cleland, a Vietnam veteran, displayed images of
Osama bin Laden and Saddam Hussein, then showed Cleland voting against homeland security legislation that had also been approved
that fall.

While Bush was not responsible for the negative ad, he did little if anything to deter this line of attack. He might conceivably
have put himself above the fray and urged an easing of partisan tensions, in much the same way that he had appealed for respect for
Muslims soon after September 11. He was a president preparing
to go to war, yet he was unwilling to put himself above the political wrangling in order to unify the nation.

Politically, the 2002 elections proved of immediate benefit to
Bush. The Republicans regained control of the Senate and increased
their majority in the House by six seats. The result was historic:
Bush became the first president since Franklin Roosevelt to pick
up seats in both houses of Congress during his first midterm election. However, over the longer run the 2002 campaign would prove
harmful to Bush, setting the stage for years of partisan acrimony
over Iraq.

The U.N. Security Council vote came next. In October, Powell
conducted what amounted to a dual series of negotiations for a
United Nations resolution on Iraq. One was with the world's other
leading powers, two of which, France and Russia, were resisting the
American initiative. Powell's other negotiations were inside the
Bush administration, where Cheney and the Pentagon sought a more
strongly worded U.N. resolution than the State Department had
proposed, with language explicitly authorizing the use of force

against Iraq. Bush remained unable to stem the deep and continuing disagreements inside his own administration.

The result was a compromise. On November 8, the Security
Council approved by a vote of fifteen to zero a resolution giving
Saddam Hussein a "final opportunity" to disclose his programs for
weapons of mass destruction and to disarm them. France agreed
to support a provision saying that Iraq would be in "material breach"
of past U.N. resolutions if it did not go along. But to get the unan-
imous vote, Bush was obliged to drop proposed language that would
have authorized "all necessary means," the common language for
the use of force, if Iraq did not comply. Thus, it was left open
whether, if Saddam balked, it would be necessary to return to the
United Nations for a second resolution before commencing military action.

• • •

The fundamental question concerning this preinvasion period is
what was motivating Bush himself. Why was he driving so determinedly toward war with Iraq and the overthrow of Saddam
Hussein's regime?

The principal reason Bush offered, both at the time and afterward, can be called the WMD argument: according to U.S. intelligence, Iraq possessed weapons of mass destruction, was in the
process of developing nuclear weapons, and had defied repeated
United Nations resolutions to terminate those programs. Before the
congressional vote in October, the CIA prepared a National Intelligence Estimate concluding that these programs were active. After
the invasion, it turned out that Saddam had misled the world into
believing he possessed WMD that, in fact, he did not have. There
seems little doubt, however, that Bush himself believed the Iraqi
leader had WMD, as did quite a few other world leaders and intelligence services.

Nevertheless, it also seems abundantly clear that Saddam's supposed WMD programs were *not* the sole reason for Bush's intense
focus on Iraq. Even according to the intelligence reports, themselves
faulty, the Iraqi regime had been acquiring the materials over a

period of years, not suddenly in 2001 and 2002, when Bush was driving toward war. That raised the question of why Bush felt he had to act when he did.

Furthermore, Bush and his aides from time to time gave other reasons to buttress their case for war. In one unguarded interview, Wolfowitz acknowledged that in making the case to the American public for war, "we settled on the one issue that everyone could agree on, which was weapons of mass destruction." Tenet wrote in his memoir that WMD was not the sole cause for the Bush administration's move against Iraq and that "in my view, I doubt it was even the principal cause."

In seeking to explain Bush's actions, some have resorted to armchair psychology. In one version, Bush was said to have been seeking vengeance against Saddam Hussein for an Iraqi plot to kill his father during a trip to Kuwait in 1993; the plot was uncovered by Kuwaiti intelligence and believed by the Clinton administration. In another version, Bush was said to harbor oedipal resentments toward his father and was seeking to demonstrate that he was able to topple Saddam when his father chose not to.

Such theories are entertaining but speculative and inadequate. The real explanations lie in the realm of policy, strategy, and worldviews. Bush seems to have agreed with many (though not all) of the reasons for war advanced by the hawks around him, including Cheney, Rumsfeld, and neoconservative officials such as Wolfowitz and Lewis (Scooter) Libby, the vice president's chief of staff. The hawks had been lobbying for action against Iraq since immediately after September 11.

Bush rejected some of their arguments. In particular, Cheney and other hawks drew direct connections between Saddam Hussein and al-Qaeda and sought to blame Iraq for the September 11 attacks, although the CIA found no evidence of such links. According to Rice, at one point Cheney arranged for Libby to brief the president on the evidence. Bush listened and then said, "You just keep on digging." In his own statements, Bush avoided trying to link Saddam to September 11.

He was much more willing to embrace the hawks' belief that Saddam Hussein was a uniquely "bad guy," a tyrannical leader who should be toppled from power because of his human rights abuses and severe political repression. Bush's father had flirted with this line of argument before the Persian Gulf War, and the younger Bush made similar claims. But this view also seems more like a secondary justification for war, since Saddam's macabre abuses had gone on for decades, and it was difficult to make the case that they were unique when compared with those of regimes such as North Korea.

Further, Bush seemed to be influenced by the hawks' belief in the importance of demonstrating America's continuing military power, especially in the Middle East. Cheney and several other administration officials had served in the Pentagon during the Gulf War, and they had witnessed how, in the immediate aftermath of that conflict, other nations in the Middle East either rushed to support the United States or avoided antagonizing it. Bush and the hawks also hoped that a successful campaign against Iraq might prompt other countries with growing nuclear capabilities, like North Korea, Iran, and Libya, to abandon their programs. This view was vindicated in the case of Libya, to Bush's considerable satisfaction; Muammar Gadhafi began to give up his nuclear program in the year after the American invasion of Iraq.

The justification for war that Bush wholeheartedly shared with Cheney, the other hawks, and Rice was that Saddam Hussein should no longer be allowed to remain in power because he might someday provide weapons of mass destruction to terrorists. This was their collective, post–September 11 mind-set and their justification for war in its essence. Under this line of thinking, it did not matter that there was no evidence the Iraqi leader had ties to al-Qaeda or any involvement in the attack on the World Trade Center, because Saddam and al-Qaeda might somehow find each other in the future. Nor did it matter that Saddam's regime and his behavior had changed little over the previous decade. September 11 itself was believed to have changed the situation, turning the same Iraq and the same Saddam Hussein into a greater threat. Many challenged this theory, raising fundamental questions about its validity. (For example, even if Saddam possessed weapons of mass destruction and even if he would consider giving them to al-Qaeda, might not a policy of deterrence cause him, in the interests of self-preservation, to decide against doing so?) But it seems clear that this line of argument reflected what Bush believed.

In Tenet's account, Bush and his incoming team had originally underestimated the threat from terrorism because none of them had been in government at the time of the al-Qaeda attacks of the 1990s. After the planes hit the World Trade Center towers, however, the opposite was true. Bush and many of those around him feared that there might be another al-Qaeda attack and that they would be blamed for having failed to prevent it.

Having experienced that day, they had become convinced that previous rules and long-standing doctrines no longer applied. Cheney dismissed Scowcroft's *Wall Street Journal* article as reflecting a "pre-9/11 mindset." Bush fully agreed. "Before 9/11, Saddam was a problem America might have been able to manage," he later wrote. "Through the lens of the post-9/11 world, my view changed. . . . The lesson of 9/11 was that if we waited for a danger to fully materialize, we would have waited too long."

• • •

Once Bush won the congressional and U.N. Security Council resolutions in the fall of 2002, the momentum of events moved steadily toward war. Saddam Hussein might have averted it by ending his charade and acknowledging that he didn't have the nuclear weapons program most governments thought he had. Chances are that Bush would not have believed him, even after the most intrusive inspections inside Iraq; U.S. intelligence had been saying otherwise. In December, Bush asked the CIA for a briefing to help prepare the case he could make to the American public about Iraq's weapons of mass destruction, and Tenet, in what he later claimed was an offhand comment, infamously said that the case was a "slam dunk." A few years later, after the war did not turn out well and no WMD were found, Tenet came to believe that Bush and Cheney used the "slam dunk" line to shift the blame to the CIA for the war they had been determined to wage.

Throughout the winter Bush ordered a steady series of deployments to Kuwait and other locations near Iraq. This buildup might have itself persuaded Saddam to back down, but he apparently misjudged. After he was captured in late 2003, Saddam told FBI debriefers that he had not believed the United States would carry through on its threats to disarm him.

Nevertheless, while the mobilization failed to convince Saddam, it contributed to the momentum toward war. Bush and his aides recognized that the troops could not sustain the mobilization for a long period. "It wasn't possible just to stand still, since doing so would leave our forces vulnerable in-theater without sufficient logistical support," Rice reflected afterward.

Rumsfeld had goaded the military to develop a war plan based on speed, mobility, and fewer troops, effectively discarding the "Powell doctrine" of the previous two decades that called for the use of overwhelming force. In invading Iraq, Bush would eventually dispatch approximately 240,000 American troops, fewer than half the number his father had sent in the Persian Gulf War. Bush stayed in close touch with the developing military preparations but paid far less attention to "softer" issues such as how to maintain stability outside the fighting areas and in the postwar period. In early 2003, Rice arranged a military briefing for the president on the subject of "rear-area security"—dealing with Iraqi civilians behind the lines while the fighting continued. Bush opened the session by telling the generals: "This is something Condi has wanted to talk about." Rice felt that after the president's introduction, which seemed to distance himself from the issue, the military no longer took the meeting seriously.

. . .

During the buildup of forces, Bush attempted once again to obtain some sort of United Nations authorization for the use of force, the issue left open after the Security Council resolution in November. He assigned Powell, the member of his administration with the highest standing in the international community, to present to the United Nations an overview of the evidence against Iraq. The secretary of state did so on February 5, 2003, based on the CIA's flawed intelligence. To skeptical European governments, it was not convincing. In short order, the powerful trio of President Jacques Chirac of France, Chancellor Gerhard Schroeder of Germany, and President Vladimir Putin of Russia joined together in opposition to military action in Iraq.

Nevertheless, Bush decided to ask the U.N. Security Council to approve a second resolution, stating that Iraq had not complied with the earlier one and specifically authorizing the use of force to compel it to do so. The position of the United States was that no such resolution was necessary because Iraq had failed to comply with the earlier resolution. But Bush went back to the U.N. at the behest of Tony Blair, whose government seemed to be in jeopardy because of his support for military action.

Bush, Rice, and Powell were hoping to persuade France and Russia to abstain from the resolution rather than veto it and then to win support for military action from most of the other nations on the fifteen-member Security Council. They tried, but did not even come close, and the failures underscored the lack of international support for military action. Bush had taken office promising to improve America's ties with Latin America, but the leaders of Mexico and Chile turned down his personal appeals. He had worked hard to develop a relationship with President Pervez Musharraf of Pakistan, but Musharraf, too, rebuffed Bush's pleas. It was a stinging diplomatic defeat for the United States and for Bush.

On March 16, as it became clear that he could not line up the votes, Bush met Blair and another ally, Prime Minister José María Aznar of Spain, in the Azores and decided it was time to abandon the effort. If the United Nations would not approve a second resolution, there would be military action without one. They would instead go to war with a "coalition of the willing." Bush wasted little time. The following day, the United States withdrew its Security Council resolution and Bush, in a televised address, issued a final ultimatum to Saddam Hussein to leave the country within forty-eight hours or face an attack. The Iraqi leader stayed put.

Bush made one last-minute effort to avoid war, seeking instead to assassinate Saddam. The CIA reported it had gotten a tip that the Iraqi leader was sleeping at Dora Farms near Baghdad. The Bush team ordered warplanes to bomb the site, but it turned out that Saddam hadn't been there. Years later, Bush offered a summary of what happened that underscored his deeper bitterness about intelligence failures: "The operation was a harbinger of things to come. Our intent was right. The pilots performed bravely. But the intelligence was wrong."

. . .

The military invasion was launched on the following day, March 20. The campaign against Iraqi forces went as smoothly and quickly as Bush, Rumsfeld, and U.S. military leaders had all planned. Within three weeks, American troops captured Baghdad. Saddam Hussein fled into hiding. As a small crowd of Iraqis cheered, an American M-88 tow truck, equipped with a crane, tore down a large statue of Saddam in the capital.

Bush was exhilarated, his mood triumphal—unwisely so, by his own later acknowledgment. In the weeks following the fall of Baghdad, his public appearances took on a jaunty, swaggering tone. On May 1, guided by navy pilots, he landed a military jet aboard the aircraft carrier USS *Abraham Lincoln* and announced the end of combat operations in Iraq. Behind him, in a location perfectly lined up for television cameras, was a large banner that read MISSION ACCOMPLISHED. Bush insisted he hadn't known this sign would be there and that this was the work of his staff. Years later, in his memoir, Bush admitted, "It was a big mistake."

. . .

America's mission in Iraq, it turned out, was far from over. In the coming months Iraq descended into sporadic looting and disorder, then to wider chaos, and then to an insurgency against American forces and to sectarian conflict that verged on civil war. It would be eight and a half more years before American troops left Iraq, and they left behind a country less stable and far less oriented to American policies in the Middle East than the Bush team had envisioned when they launched the war. There was one notable success: in December 2003, American forces found Saddam Hussein hiding in a hole not far from his ancestral home in Tikrit. But despite searching the country intensively, they could find no evidence of weapons of mass destruction or of an active program to produce them.

Despite the sixteen months of planning and preparation, Bush and his senior advisers had operated on a series of faulty assumptions. This series of misjudgments, taken together, turned the Iraq War into a strategic mistake of historic proportions.

The failed diplomacy at the United Nations was the result of these misjudgments. Throughout the administration's campaign against Saddam Hussein, it was assumed that America's international support would be greater than it turned out to be. When allies in Europe and friendly governments elsewhere initially opposed the war, Bush's advisers believed that, in the end, they would line up behind the United States, or at least not openly oppose it. Even in the final weeks before war, the administration overestimated how many countries would be willing to support it at the United Nations.

Bush and his team also vastly underestimated the costs and duration of the war. Before the conflict started, Lawrence Lindsey was pilloried for estimating that the war might cost as much as $100 billion. In fact, that supposedly high estimate was too low by a factor of twenty: in 2013, ten years after the start of the military intervention in Iraq, direct U.S. government expenditures for the war had surpassed $2 trillion. At the time the war started, the estimates of how long the United States would remain in Iraq were in the range of a couple of years. Instead, American troops stayed in Iraq for nearly nine years, suffered 4,500 fatalities, and departed under circumstances that fell far short of the stable, democratic Iraq that Bush had envisioned.

One major reason for these faulty estimates was a misjudgment about how Iraqis would respond after the invasion. Four days before the start of the war, in an interview on *Meet the Press*, Cheney was asked whether he thought the American people were prepared for a long, costly, and bloody battle with significant U.S. casualties. "I really don't think it's likely to unfold that way, because I really do believe that we will be greeted as liberators," he replied. There is no sign that Bush disagreed with this judgment. Cheney's assertion was arguably valid for some Iraqis for a short time, in the weeks immediately following the fall of Baghdad. After that, however, the "greeted-as-liberators" line rang increasingly hollow, as the United States found itself unable to stabilize Iraq.

The reason for this instability was another misjudgment. Bush and his team failed to plan properly for postwar operations in Iraq. The United States simply did not have enough troops to keep things calm. The forces that were there were not prepared for what they were about to face. Before the war, the Pentagon and the State Department had engaged in continual bickering over the reconstruction of Iraq and its political leadership after Saddam Hussein. As was often true in his first years in the White House, Bush proved unable to gauge the depth or the impact of the personal and ideological battles being waged beneath him.

Years later, Bush acknowledged ruefully that, even though he thought the United States was prepared to deal with postwar Iraq, "our nation building capabilities were limited, and no one knew for sure what needs would arise." He had relied on assurances from Rumsfeld and military leaders that the U.S. troop levels for postwar Iraq were sufficient. He had, in fact, relied on his advisers for many of his judgments about war with Iraq. One of the tasks of an American president, however, is to be skeptical of the advice he is getting and to sense when the predictions of what will come are governed more by hope than by reality.

6

Reelection and Its Unhappy Aftermath

George W. Bush had arrived in the White House as a novice in foreign policy but a very old hand at electoral politics. He had begun working in politics the year after his college graduation and had helped run several Senate and House races, his father's three presidential campaigns, his own two gubernatorial campaigns, and his presidential campaign in 2000. It was easy to underestimate him as a politician, and he liked it that way. Bush knew all the drills: how to deflect an opponent's charges, how to counterattack, how to stay on message.

The presidential election of 2004 would be his last campaign, and he wanted to leave nothing to chance. Just after New Year's Day in 2003, he sat down at his Texas ranch with Karl Rove to start planning his reelection campaign. Within months, they were deep into strategy: which states to go after and which themes to emphasize. After the start of the war in Iraq, Rove decided that the campaign should focus on portraying Bush as a "strong wartime leader."

In the summer of 2003, Vice President Dick Cheney told Bush at one of their weekly lunches that he would be willing to step aside the following year if Bush wanted a different running mate on the ticket. Cheney had become a lightning rod for criticism of the administration, and Bush did not immediately dismiss this offer, conferring briefly with close aides about replacing Cheney with Bill Frist, the Senate majority leader. Bush quickly decided, however, that while Cheney might be a political target in the campaign, he wanted Cheney as his vice president in the second term.

At first, Bush hoped to run against Howard Dean, the former governor of Vermont, who emerged as an early front-runner for the Democratic nomination by courting the party's vocal antiwar constituencies. Bush had known Dean when they were both governors and considered him shrill and undisciplined. To Bush's disappointment, Dean's candidacy collapsed, and Senator John Kerry of Massachusetts, whom he considered a more formidable opponent, was chosen as the Democratic nominee.

. . .

Throughout Bush's first term, amid the tumult of the overseas wars and antiterrorism measures, he had been attempting to establish a record at home on which he could run for reelection as a nondoctrinaire Republican.

Bush's tax cuts formed the core of his legacy in domestic policy, and his actions on environmental and right-to-life issues furthered the judgment of him as a president who stood decidedly to the right on the political spectrum. There were, however, a number of areas of domestic policy where Bush departed from conservative orthodoxy and from the unyielding approach he had displayed when he first took office. In some cases, he reluctantly accepted legislation sponsored by the Democrats. In other instances, he worked out compromises with the Democrats or put forward initiatives of his own that did not fit his conservative image.

In July 2002, Bush signed into law a bill that considerably strengthened the ability of the federal government to investigate and prosecute corporate fraud. The legislation, sponsored by Democratic senator Paul Sarbanes and Republican representative Michael Oxley, was a congressional response to a series of corporate and accounting scandals. Enron, the Texas energy conglomerate whose chairman, Kenneth Lay, was a friend of Bush and a leading campaign contributor, had filed for bankruptcy in late 2001, and Worldcom, a prominent telecommunications firm, had similarly sought bankruptcy protection a half year later. Bush had fought many of the central provisions of the legislation until three weeks before he signed it, but then, in the wake of the collapse of Worldcom, he reversed course and decided to endorse the measure. For years afterward, business groups and libertarian conservative organizations complained about the impact of Sarbanes-Oxley and called for its repeal, maintaining that its reporting requirements were too onerous and that it was a symbol of an overly intrusive federal government.

Bush's decision to expand Medicare angered conservatives even more. In the fall of 2003, he signed legislation under which Medicare began to pay for prescription drugs, thus establishing a new entitlement (called Medicare Part D) that even supporters acknowledged would be extraordinarily costly. It amounted to the biggest expansion of the Medicare program since its creation in 1965.

Indeed, whenever Bush spoke about the new prescription-drug benefit, his language sounded like that of a conventional liberal. He portrayed his program as an effort to meet social needs and as a progressive advance for the welfare state. "Medicare's most antiquated feature was that it did not cover prescription drugs," he wrote in his memoir. "The program would pay $28,000 for ulcer surgery, but not $500 a year for pills that would prevent most ulcers. I was struck by the stories of older Americans who had to choose between buying groceries and medicine."

Yet beyond these sympathies, Bush may also have been influenced by political and economic factors. He proposed the expansion of Medicare just as he was preparing to run for reelection. America's leading pharmaceutical companies, which contribute heavily to political campaigns, strongly supported the new drug benefit; so did the American Association of Retired Persons (AARP), the principal organization for the elderly, an important electoral constituency.

Moreover, Bush initially viewed the new drug benefit as a means of accomplishing one of his broader conservative goals: the privatization of America's social programs. His original proposal would have required those seeking prescription drug subsidies to give up their government-run Medicare and instead enroll in private insurance programs for all of their health care. "By delivering the drug benefit through private insurance plans that compete for seniors' business, we could inject market forces into the health care system," Bush argued.

Republican congressional leaders told Bush there was no way such a privatization measure could win passage, because Democrats would never support a change in the fundamental nature of Medicare. Bush then retreated, proposing legislation under which the overall Medicare program would remain unchanged but for the addition of a new drug benefit run by private insurers. Yet even this narrower legislation ran into intense opposition in Congress: most Democrats refused to support an augmented role for private insurers, while conservative Republicans were loath to create a new drug benefit at all. The vote in Congress was so close that it required extraordinary tactics by Speaker of the House Dennis Hastert and by Bush himself to push the bill through. The bill was rejected in an initial House vote at three o'clock one morning. Instead of accepting the result, Hastert kept the vote open while Bush made a few phone calls in the predawn hours to wavering Republicans. By early morning, the result was reversed: the House approved the bill 220 to 215, and the drug benefit became law.

Bush launched one other social initiative with enduring impact: a campaign of unprecedented scope and with significant U.S. government funding to combat AIDS in Africa. Under his plan, the President's Emergency Plan for AIDS Relief (PEPFAR), the U.S. government gave an initial $15 billion over five years to pay the costs for prevention and treatment of AIDS, a sum vastly larger than that contributed by other nations or by the Clinton administration. Much of the money went toward the purchase of antiretroviral drugs. A common assumption at the time was that antiretroviral drugs would not be effective in Africa, because many AIDS victims there would not be able to take the drugs on the regular, specific timetable that is required. The PEPFAR program proved this assumption to be wrong.

As with Bush's expansion of Medicare, there may have been considerations of timing and of domestic politics. Although American conservatives had for years attacked the general concept of foreign aid, the specific idea of combating AIDS in Africa was especially popular with evangelical Christians. Moreover, Bush announced the PEPFAR program only a few weeks before the invasion of Iraq; it thus served as a reminder, amid the acrimony over the war, that the United States could use its power as a force for good in the world.

Nevertheless, it also seems clear that in establishing the PEP-FAR program, domestic political considerations were not paramount and that Bush was motivated primarily by altruistic considerations. He had long claimed to represent a new form of compassionate conservatism, and the AIDS program was an instance where he sought to make this slogan a reality. He maintained interest in PEPFAR throughout his presidency. The Bush administration's budget planners argued against such a large commitment of money for the program, but Bush brushed aside their concerns. Late in his presidency, as the original five-year authorization ran out, he proposed doubling the money to $30 billion over the following five years. Eventually, Congress (then controlled by the Democrats) approved that amount and more.

Bush's program engendered a series of side controversies. Some conservatives were unhappy that the AIDS program was distributing condoms. Liberals, on the other hand, ridiculed the part of the program that promoted abstinence. Meanwhile, consumer groups complained that PEPFAR was a boon to the pharmaceutical industry because it favored brand-name drugs over their generic counterparts. Still, Bush persevered, continuing to give high-level support, avoiding entanglement in these subsidiary issues. In time, Bush's program became the largest single-nation health initiative in the world; by 2012, PEPFAR would provide antiretroviral drugs for more than 4.5 million people.

· · ·

The biggest problem confronting Bush in his reelection campaign was that Iraq was increasingly turning into a disaster. The MISSION ACCOMPLISHED banner of May 2003 came back to haunt him. What began as an outbreak of looting after American troops entered Baghdad descended into wider chaos and violence across the country. There were simply not enough American troops to maintain order.

To stabilize the situation, Bush appointed L. Paul Bremer to head the new Coalition Provisional Authority with full administrative powers to govern Iraq until a new government could be formed. However, Bremer soon compounded the problems by issuing orders to disband the Iraqi army and to deny government jobs to all members of the Ba'ath Party, which had ruled the country under Saddam Hussein. The result was that many thousands of Iraqis, some of them armed, were left without jobs or a stake in a future government. In August 2003, a massive bomb at the U.N. headquarters in Baghdad killed the U.N.'s special representative Sergio Vieira de Mello, and two months later Deputy Secretary of Defense Paul Wolfowitz barely escaped an attack in which rockets were fired at his Baghdad hotel. Worst of all for Bush, American forces found no weapons of mass destruction. Neither did other investigators over the following months and years. Saddam Hussein, it appeared, had been bluffing. Thus, the principal reason Bush had cited as justification for the war turned out to have been an illusion.

In public, Bush and his aides often sought to minimize the problems. At the Pentagon, Donald Rumsfeld at first brushed off the looting with the quip, "Stuff happens." Even as it became increasingly clear that organized groups were targeting the U.S. troops in an effort to dislodge them from Iraq, Rumsfeld for a time disputed the notion that America faced an "insurgency" in Iraq. For his own part, Bush taunted those in Iraq who sought to force the Americans out of the country. "My answer is: Bring 'em on," he said. Amid the intensifying violence, Bush resisted sending more troops to Iraq because he did not want to reinforce the impression of an imperial America. But that strategy backfired; Bush ruefully acknowledged years later that it turned out that "the Iraqi people's desire for security trumped their aversion to empire."

Bush's fortunes got a huge boost in the final weeks of 2003, when Saddam Hussein was captured. Photographs of the bedraggled leader were soon displayed around the world, particularly inside

Iraq, where they served as proof that there would be no comeback. Saddam Hussein's regime was officially finished; the tyrant had been humbled. Within months, however, the impact of that image was soon overwhelmed by another set of photographs, ones that cast America's occupation of Iraq in such a negative light that, as Condoleezza Rice later admitted, "We never recovered fully." A group of U.S. soldiers had taken photos inside the infamous Abu Ghraib prison that showed Iraqi prisoners forced into humiliating poses, sometimes hooded or without clothes, while their American guards gloated.

Rumsfeld had informed the president about reports of mistreatment of prisoners at Abu Ghraib, but Bush had not seen the graphic images until the day they appeared on American television. He was appalled. "I considered it a low point of my presidency," he wrote. He also felt blindsided, suddenly faced with an intense controversy he didn't know was coming. Amid the furor that erupted, Rumsfeld twice submitted his resignation as defense secretary. Bush considered accepting it but instead sent the vice president to the Pentagon to plead with Rumsfeld to stay on the job. Bush asserted that the reasons he kept Rumsfeld on were that he had no immediate replacement and didn't want to change defense secretaries in the middle of a war. One additional factor he didn't mention was the timing: the Abu Ghraib scandal broke in the middle of an election year. Replacing Rumsfeld would have amounted to admitting that there was a problem in leadership in the wartime Pentagon; it would also have made it appear that the Bush administration was in disarray.

In private, Bush was coming to that latter conclusion on his own. He was upset by the skirmishing within his foreign-policy team, both at the top, where Cheney disagreed regularly with Powell and Rice sparred with Rumsfeld, and at lower levels, where the subordinates of these officials waged proxy battles. At roughly the same time as the Abu Ghraib abuses came to light, Powell informed Bush he wanted to step down. Bush persuaded him to stay on until after the election, but the president also decided he needed a wholesale shake-up of the national security team in his second term.

The most dramatic of the battles within the administration was hidden from public view at the time. It concerned the National Security Agency's Terrorist Surveillance Program, the extensive monitoring instituted soon after September 11, which had to be reauthorized every forty-five days. In the early months of 2004, Justice Department lawyers, eventually supported by Deputy Attorney General James Comey, decided that several key aspects of the NSA program were illegal; they could not be justified under existing laws or the Constitution.

Cheney had played a large role in creating the program and had remained closely involved in it. In early March, as the next reauthorization deadline loomed, the vice president and his legal adviser David Addington engaged in a tense confrontation with the Justice Department lawyers. Cheney tried but failed to overcome the objections of Comey and his aides. At the time, Attorney General John Ashcroft lay seriously ill in a Washington hospital. Bush dispatched White House chief of staff Andrew Card and White House counsel Alberto Gonzales to Ashcroft's hospital room, seeking to ask the attorney general, barely conscious, to approve a continuation of the program. But Comey and two Justice Department lawyers beat the White House aides to the hospital and told the semiconscious attorney general what was happening. Ashcroft spurned the White House requests.

The issue went up to Bush, who at first decided to invoke his own presidential powers to overrule the Justice Department and extend the NSA surveillance. However, the Justice Department was by this time in open revolt. Comey informed the White House that he would resign if Bush unilaterally authorized the program. Government lawyers, not just at the Justice Department but also at the FBI and CIA, said that they would resign along with Comey; their numbers quickly swelled to two dozen, including some of Bush's own political appointees. In what would have been the most damaging resignation of all, FBI director Robert Mueller said he, too, would leave if Bush overrode the Justice Department.

Bush was thus confronted with the prospect of mass resignations that would almost certainly have drawn comparisons to Richard

Nixon's "Saturday Night Massacre" during Watergate. He backed down, agreeing to make changes in the component of the NSA program to which the Justice Department objected. Comey and the other officials stayed on.

In the aftermath, Bush was angry with his subordinates. Although the dispute between Cheney and the Justice Department had been brewing for weeks, he said no one had informed him of it until the final days. "I made clear to my advisers that I never wanted to be blindsided like that again," he later wrote.

• • •

Despite the turmoil inside his administration, Bush waged a smooth and competent reelection campaign. John Kerry denounced Bush for his decision to invade Iraq and for the overzealous handling of his campaign against terrorism. Kerry and many other Democrats assumed that the Massachusetts senator's military service in Vietnam would establish his credentials and experience on national security, an area where Democrats had long proved vulnerable.

Bush was too experienced a politician to let Kerry set his own narrative for the campaign without challenge. In March, the Bush team seized the offensive. Kerry was preparing to give a speech in West Virginia in which he planned to attack Bush for his lack of support for veterans. The day before the speech, the Bush team aired a television spot called "Troops," attacking Kerry for having voted against a funding bill that provided $87 billion for American troops in Afghanistan and Iraq. The suggestion was that Kerry was a typical antiwar liberal.

Kerry took the bait. At the West Virginia event, he defended himself by pointing out that it was merely one of a series of procedural votes he cast on the measure. "I actually did vote for the $87 billion before I voted against it," he inartfully explained. As soon as Bush heard those words, he called Rove. "There's our opening," Bush said. Kerry had handed Bush and his team the theme they exploited throughout the general-election campaign: that Kerry was a flip-flopper who failed to take clear stands on issues and to stick with them.

During the general-election campaign, Bush talked about his domestic agenda for his second term. He said he wanted to reform Social Security by partially privatizing individual accounts and to reform the immigration system by offering a path to citizenship to undocumented immigrants. In turn, Kerry sought to keep the focus on Bush's handling of the Iraq War.

Bizarrely, however, the campaign became swept up in old issues stemming from the Vietnam War. Bush's opponents once again raised old questions about Bush's combat-free service in the National Guard. Meanwhile, at the height of the campaign a murky pro-Bush group, Swift Boat Veterans for Truth, ran television spots attacking Kerry's war record and his patriotism. Even Senator John McCain of Arizona, while supporting Bush, called the ads deplorable and said they reminded him of Bush's attacks on him in the 2000 Republican primaries. Bush disavowed the Swift Boat ads, asserting that they were made by an independent group that was not connected to his reelection campaign. He subsequently made a mild plea, unheeded, for a ban on advertising by all independent groups. Writing years later, Rove observed defiantly, "I had no role in any of it, though the Swifties did a damn good job."

Ultimately, the Bush campaign succeeded in portraying the president as down-to-earth and Kerry as an elitist out of touch with the moods and lifestyles of ordinary Americans, even though, by family background, income, and education, Bush qualified as an elitist as much as Kerry did, if not more so. At the simplest level, Kerry carried himself with patrician bearing, while Bush did not. Bush had long ago learned the lessons from his congressional campaign in 1978, when his successful opponent depicted him an Easterner from Andover and Yale. By 2004, George W. Bush was especially adept at putting himself forward as a good ol' boy, joking, wisecracking, and happy to sit down over a (nonalcoholic) beer.

By historical standards the Bush-Kerry election was close, not as close as that four years earlier but tighter than in most presidential years. On Election Day, exit polls appeared to show that Kerry was winning. When the actual votes came in later that night, they showed that many of the exit polls had been wrong. By the next morning, when Bush was declared to have won the state of Ohio with its twenty electoral votes, Kerry conceded defeat.

• • •

In his postelection news conference, Bush served notice that he intended to accomplish a lot in his second term. He said he planned to move ahead with far-reaching changes in the Social Security system and immigration reform. "I earned capital in the campaign, political capital, and now I intend to spend it," he said.

Bush also moved quickly to reshape his national security team. He appointed Rice, his closest aide, as secretary of state, and elevated Rice's former deputy Steven Hadley to national security adviser. With these actions, Bush established his personal control over foreign policy. Powell, who had told the president that he planned to step down as secretary of state after the November elections, had a momentary change of heart and suggested he would like to stay on the job, but Bush rebuffed his offer. Several other participants in the bureaucratic battles of the first term, such as Deputy Secretary of State Richard Armitage and Deputy Secretary of Defense Paul Wolfowitz, either resigned or were moved to other jobs.

On January 20, 2005, in his second inaugural address, Bush set forth a vision of America's role in the world that was breathtaking in ambition. The focus was on spreading democracy across the globe. In a relatively brief speech, he invoked the words "freedom," "free," and "liberty" forty-nine times. "It is the policy of the United States to seek and support the growth of democratic movements and institutions in every nation and culture, with the ultimate goal of ending tyranny in our world," he declared. Since he had not described American policy in such broad terms early in his presidency, it was fair to wonder whether Bush was, in effect, retrospectively seeking to justify the war in Iraq as an effort to promote freedom rather than to deal with the supposed weapons of mass destruction that were never found.

The next day, *New York Times* columnist William Safire observed that Bush "now drives his critics batty by exuding a buoyant confidence reminiscent of Truman and F.D.R." Few realized it, but at that moment, on the first days of his second term, Bush's presidency was probably at its apex in its ambition, influence, and public support. It was about to begin a long slide downhill.

• • •

Bush's first defeat came with Social Security. Throughout the late winter and spring of 2005, he barnstormed the country, making the case that Americans should be allowed to invest their Social Security earnings in private accounts. But this campaign went nowhere; Bush had misjudged both the public's appetite for Social Security reform and his ability to persuade the electorate.

He knew he held only a slim majority in the country, but his hope was to get Social Security privatization through Congress with the same lightning speed that he had pushed through his tax cuts in 2001. Back then, congressional Republicans had united to support the tax cuts, while the Democrats were divided; the tax measure passed with the help of Democratic defections. But when it came to the Social Security proposal, these political dynamics were reversed: Democrats rapidly joined together in determined opposition, while congressional Republicans were lukewarm in their support. Few Republicans wanted to be recorded as voting against the existing system, when such a vote could pose a problem in the next congressional elections. In a version of political hot potato, House members urged that a vote be put off until after action by the Senate, while Senate Republicans wanted the House to go first. As a result, Bush's plan to overhaul Social Security died a slow death. It was not even brought to a vote: in the fall of 2005, House Republican leaders told Bush they had decided to move on to other issues.

• • •

In late summer, Bush's political fortunes were dealt another severe blow. A tropical storm formed in the Atlantic and moved toward the American mainland, growing into Hurricane Katrina. As it passed over Florida and headed across the Gulf of Mexico, it gathered strength to become a rare category five hurricane, one of the worst storms in a century. Katrina hit New Orleans with full force: the levees broke; the city flooded; and chaos and looting broke out on the streets. Overall, Katrina, which caused more than 1,800 deaths, destroyed at least 300,000 homes, and caused roughly $100 billion in property damage, was the most expensive storm in American history.

By his own subsequent admission, Bush moved too slowly in marshaling the full force of the federal government to deal with the storm. When he sought to send federal troops to help New Orleans, he ran into bureaucratic resistance both from state officials in Louisiana and from the Pentagon. Governor Kathleen Blanco of Louisiana did not want the military deployment, because it meant she would have to surrender control over her state's National Guard forces. Rumsfeld was loath to send American forces, then in the midst of two ongoing wars, to carry out a domestic mission for which they had not been trained. For days, with New Orleans in growing turmoil, Bush was unable to overcome these obstacles. Finally, after failing to win the governor's support, he sent more than seven thousand active-duty troops anyway, although, in deference to local sensitivities, they were given no law-enforcement powers, and their army commander was obliged to report to the governor on anything relating to the National Guard.

These delays were compounded by major problems in the Federal Emergency Management Agency (FEMA), whose leadership had been handed over to Bush's political appointees. Bush's first director had been Joseph Allbaugh, a longtime friend and colleague who had served as chief of staff when Bush was governor of Texas. Allbaugh left when FEMA was turned from an independent agency into a part of the newly created Department of Homeland Security. As his successor, Allbaugh recommended his own longtime friend Michael Brown, who had been serving as FEMA's general counsel. Before joining the administration, Brown's primary experience had been as judges and stewards commissioner for the International Arabian Horse Association. Even Karl Rove, not generally opposed to appointments of Bush's political supporters, had argued that Brown lacked the qualifications to run FEMA. Bush appointed him anyway. During Hurricane Katrina, FEMA's responses were so slow that Secretary of Homeland Security Michael Chertoff finally asked Bush to relieve Brown of his responsibilities. Bush brought in a replacement to take charge of the response to Katrina, and Brown soon resigned.

Bush displayed a poor sense of public relations in dealing with the storm. Early on, he allowed himself to be photographed on Air Force One looking down at the storm damage as he flew over Louisiana without stopping there. There were good reasons to avoid making an on-the-ground visit, he maintained: he did not want to distract attention from the relief efforts. Yet the photo made him appear detached and distant, precisely the opposite of the perception Bush had established with his visit to Ground Zero in New York City after September 11. A few days later, Bush made things much worse. Seeking to boost morale in FEMA and its director, he declared in front of reporters, "Brownie, you're doing a heck of a job!" Even more than the airplane photo, those eight words became an enduring symbol of the administration's failure.

Years later, Bush acknowledged his mishandling of Katrina. "I prided myself on my ability to make crisp and effective decisions," he wrote. "Yet in the days after Katrina, that didn't happen. The problem was not that I made the wrong decisions. It was that I took too long to decide."

. . .

On July 1, 2005, Supreme Court Justice Sandra Day O'Connor announced her decision to step down from the seat she had occupied for twenty-four years. That gave Bush a chance to shape the future of the Court. Replacing O'Connor, however, turned into a prolonged process that included another damaging political defeat for the president.

After three weeks of candidate vetting, Bush settled on the nominee he wanted: John G. Roberts, a judge on the U.S. Court of Appeals for the District of Columbia Circuit, the nation's most powerful appeals court. Roberts's elite legal and conservative credentials were strong: he had graduated from Harvard College and

Harvard Law School, served as a Supreme Court law clerk, and rose to become principal deputy U.S. solicitor general. He had argued more than three dozen cases before the Supreme Court. Linda Greenhouse, the *New York Times*'s Supreme Court correspondent, praised him at the time of his appointment as a jurist "deeply anchored in the trajectory of modern constitutional law." From Bush's viewpoint, Roberts possessed one other noteworthy asset: he was only fifty years old, young enough potentially to serve on the Court for three decades or more.

Then the surprises began. While Roberts was awaiting his nomination hearings, Chief Justice William H. Rehnquist, who had thyroid cancer, suddenly died. That opened a second vacancy. Bush quickly withdrew Roberts's nomination as associate justice and instead appointed him to assume Rehnquist's place as chief justice. For the second open seat, Bush chose a close White House aide whose friendship dated back to their years in Texas together: White House counsel Harriet Miers, who had once been Bush's personal lawyer.

Not surprisingly, the Miers appointment elicited criticism from liberals and Democrats. Yet it also drew surprising and impassioned opposition from conservatives. The Republican right had long complained that too many Republican appointees, such as William Brennan, John Paul Stevens, David Souter, and O'Connor herself, had turned out to be more moderate or liberal than expected. Miers had virtually no track record from which to glean her underlying beliefs on constitutional issues. Her principal qualification for the job was her close association with Bush. However, that would have little meaning at all after he left the White House.

Bush sought to overcome the conservatives' objections, accusing his critics of elitism because Miers had graduated from Southern Methodist University Law School rather than Harvard or Yale. The conservative columnist Charles Krauthammer, who for years had been one of Bush's strongest defenders, offered a devastating response to this argument. "This is not about the Ivy League," he wrote. "The issue is not the *venue* of Miers's constitutional scholarship, experience and engagement. The issue is their nonexistence."

After three weeks of such criticism, Miers asked Bush to with-draw her nomination. Bush quickly went along. To take her place, he nominated Judge Samuel Alito of the U.S. Court of Appeals for the Third Circuit, who was, like Roberts, an experienced, identifi-ably conservative jurist. Alito won confirmation by the relatively narrow margin of fifty-eight to forty-two, with the vote overwhelm-ingly along partisan lines.

Once Roberts and Alito were sworn in, they were in position to move the court in a more conservative direction, and the votes they would cast became part of Bush's long-term legacy. Yet in the short run, the failure of the Miers nomination was another sign of Bush's flagging political influence, even in his own party. It dem-onstrated the growing distance between Bush and the Republi-can right, which was beginning to think beyond the Bush years. The tensions with the conservatives would burst forth once again with far greater impact during Bush's hectic final months as pres-ident.

• • •

Overseas, the situation in Iraq continued to deteriorate. Bush scored one major achievement at the beginning of 2005, when Iraqis turned out in large numbers to vote in their first free democratic election. Pictures of voters happily holding up purple fingers, indicating that they had voted, filled American newspapers and television screens. The military situation, however, remained grim. That year roughly seventy-five to eighty Americans were killed each month in Iraq and another four hundred to six hundred were wounded. Head shots of those who died were a regular staple of television and news-paper coverage, and these photos had a more lasting impact than the purple thumbprints.

At home, the rancor over the war was even greater than at the time of the invasion. With Kerry's defeat, the Democrats began to move steadily leftward, reflecting a growing antiwar sentiment. In the Senate, where prominent Democrats had years earlier voted to authorize the use of force in Iraq, there were now ever harsher attacks on Bush.

Bush's decision to launch the Iraq War gave rise to a series of investigations, mostly in Congress but also at the Justice Department. In the fall of 2005, I. Lewis "Scooter" Libby, Cheney's chief of staff, was indicted for perjury in connection with a federal investigation into the leaking of the name of intelligence official Valerie Plame. Plame's husband, a former ambassador named Joseph Wilson, had been critical of the Bush administration's prewar claim that Iraq was actively developing weapons of mass destruction. Libby's indictment was a blow to the vice president and set the stage for a frosty dispute between Bush and Cheney in their final days in the White House.

Looking back at the series of debacles in late 2005, including Hurricane Katrina, the failure of his proposal on Social Security, and the unending violence in Iraq, Bush summarized mordantly: "Just a year earlier, I had won reelection with more votes than any candidate in history. By the end of 2005, much of my political capital was gone."

• • •

The following year was no better for Bush and in some ways worse. In the spring of 2006, the Supreme Court dealt the first severe blow to the legal underpinnings of Bush's war on terror.

Over the previous few years, quite a few of the secret programs Bush had set up after September 11 had come to light. In 2004, a CIA inspector general issued an internal report that questioned the legality of the agency's use of harsh interrogation techniques. The report leaked, and the world soon learned the meaning of the term "waterboarding." In November 2005, the *Washington Post* reported on the CIA's clandestine program of operating secret prisons ("black sites") around the world in which it held and interrogated al-Qaeda operatives. Six weeks later, the *New York Times* revealed the existence of the National Security Agency's Terrorist Surveillance Program.

Despite this series of revelations, there remained no outside constraints on Bush's counterterrorism programs. That would soon change. In a sweeping decision handed down on June 29, 2006, the

Supreme Court held that some aspects of the war on terror had been illegal and, furthermore, that contrary to the Bush administration's claims all the prisoners at Guantánamo were entitled to the protections of the Geneva Conventions. In this case, *Hamdan v. Rumsfeld*, the court ruled five to three that Bush had no authority on his own to set up new military commissions to try al-Qaeda detainees; instead, Congress should have been asked to approve the new system. Thus, the hurried and furtive White House decision making of November 2001—in which Bush signed an order for military commissions drafted by the vice president's office, ignoring an ongoing review by the cabinet agencies—had resulted in errors that caused the program to be ruled unconstitutional.

The Supreme Court decision had several far-reaching consequences. Bush was forced to go to Congress for legislation authorizing military commissions. He succeeded but only after protracted negotiations. Moreover, following the *Hamdan* decision, the CIA reviewed its interrogation programs, cut back on some but not all of the harsh techniques, and transferred all of the fourteen al-Qaeda detainees out of the "black sites" and into Guantánamo.

• • •

In Iraq, the violence not only continued through 2006 but took on an entirely new dimension. In February, the Golden Mosque in Samarra, a holy site for Shia Islam, was destroyed by two large bombs. Within months, sectarian fighting erupted between Shiites and Sunnis, while the attacks on American troops continued. The death figures told the story. American fatalities in 2006 were roughly the same as in the previous year, but the deaths of Iraqi civilians shot upward: in a single month, September 2006, more than three thousand Iraqi civilians were killed. After a visit to Iraq that fall, Rice told Bush directly: "Mr. President, what we are doing is not working—really not working. It's failing."

Inside Washington, the Iraq War was now reaching the point of crisis as the domestic opposition grew ever more intense. In the spring of 2006, a number of retired generals publicly called for the ouster of Rumsfeld, arguing that he was mismanaging the war effort and that he often rejected the advice of his military commanders. Bush once again said he would keep Rumsfeld on the job. It was in this context that he offered his long-remembered quote: "I'm the decider. And I decide what is best," he said. "And what's best is for Don Rumsfeld to remain as the secretary of defense."

In September, Mitch McConnell, the second-ranking Republican in the Senate, asked to speak with the president in private. Inside the Oval Office, he told Bush that because of his growing unpopularity the Republicans were going to lose control of the House and the Senate in the November elections. He pleaded with Bush to start withdrawing some American troops from Iraq. Bush responded that he was not going to let his policy in Iraq be determined by the polls.

McConnell's prediction proved accurate. When the results of the midterm elections came in, Bush and the Republicans suffered a resounding defeat. The Democrats took back the House of Representatives for the first time since the Gingrich revolution of 1994. Instead of dealing with dependably loyal Speaker Dennis Hastert, Bush would be obliged during his final two years in office to do business with Nancy Pelosi, a combative and tenacious liberal Democrat. The Senate changed hands, too, as the Democrats picked up six seats. The Democrats won a majority of the nation's governorships and picked up hundreds of seats in state legislatures.

Karl Rove, who had guided the Republican strategy for the 2006 campaign, later tried to blame the defeat mostly on a series of scandals involving individual Republicans in Congress rather than on Bush's policies. The election had little to do with Iraq or with Bush's handling of Katrina and Social Security, he insisted defensively.

But Bush had no illusions about what had transpired. At a news conference the day after the election, he put it succinctly: "It was a thumping."

———

7

Second-Term Changes

Immediately following the 2006 congressional elections, George W. Bush took the momentous step he had been considering for several years. He announced that Donald Rumsfeld would step down as defense secretary. As his replacement, Bush selected Robert Gates, the veteran intelligence official who had served in the George H. W. Bush administration as deputy national security adviser and as director of central intelligence.

This was not merely a personnel change at the Pentagon but a shift in the center of gravity and worldview of Bush's foreign-policy team. Gates was closely allied with the realists in George H. W. Bush's administration who had favored a balance-of-power approach over idealism and preferred cautious multilateral diplomacy to unilateralism. Over the years, he had learned the ways of national security in Washington from two former bosses, Brent Scowcroft and Zbigniew Brzezinski, who by 2006 had become the two most prominent critics within the foreign-policy community of George W. Bush's decision to invade Iraq.

The ouster of Rumsfeld was a significant blow to the power and influence of Vice President Cheney. Rumsfeld had been Cheney's close friend for decades and his steadfast ally on policy questions. Twice in the previous two years, Cheney had persuaded Bush not to let Rumsfeld go. A few days before the 2006 elections, however, Bush called the vice president aside and informed him that after Election Day he was making the change Cheney had long opposed.

It was an icy meeting. "This time the president didn't wait around after he told me he had made up his mind," Cheney wrote later. "He turned and was out the door fast."

Bush fully understood the implications for his vice president. At the end of an interview with Gates for the Pentagon job, he had asked if Gates had any further questions. Then, smiling, Bush prompted, "Cheney?," raising on his own the sensitive question of Cheney's role in the administration that Gates hadn't asked. "He is a voice, an important voice, but only one voice," the president said.

Cheney's position had already been weakened by the indictment in late 2005 of I. Lewis "Scooter" Libby, his chief of staff. With Rumsfeld's departure, the vice president became increasingly a minority voice within the administration; his hawkish views on foreign policy no longer dominated. During the final two years of his presidency, Bush would make a series of decisions, particularly on foreign policy, over Cheney's opposition.

The replacement of Rumsfeld was not so much the catalyst for a change of direction for Bush as it was the crowning moment for a change that was already under way. From the first days of Bush's second term, his administration had increasingly taken on a different tone and emphasis as the president sought to counteract the negative impact of his invasion of Iraq. He by then had strong reasons of self-interest to pursue the multilateral approaches he had forsaken earlier; in Iraq, for example, he was now eager for European aid and personnel to alleviate the chaos that had erupted after the American invasion.

At the same time, Bush was increasingly inclined to rely on his own judgments rather than those of his advisers. This shift was difficult for the public to detect, because the Iraq War was still ongoing and had greater long-term significance for the United States than any of the actions Bush took to repair the damage. Nevertheless, the initiatives Bush took in foreign policy during his second term were of considerable significance and were later praised by the Obama administration.

Beyond Bush himself, the principal agent for these changes was Secretary of State Condoleezza Rice, who on a personal level was much closer to Bush than any other member of the foreign-policy team and thus was able to win Bush's support for diplomacy where in many cases Powell was not. Their close bond also meant that Bush could use Rice as his instrument for altering the course of foreign policy that had been set under the strong influence of Cheney and Rumsfeld during the first term. Modest and deferential in the early years of the administration, Rice transformed herself into a skilled operator in the internal bureaucratic combat that was a hallmark of the Bush foreign-policy team. When Bush had first asked her to become secretary of state, she told him she wanted to run foreign policy without Rumsfeld's input. Two years later, when Bush told her he was about to replace Rumsfeld, she recorded her reaction as follows: "I could barely contain my joy." She had worked closely with Gates on Soviet policy in George H. W. Bush's White House, and the two quickly renewed their smooth relationship. Gates would later write that on virtually every foreign-policy issue, "she and I were pretty much on the same page." It was quite a contrast to the frosty relationship between Rice and Rumsfeld.

In some instances, the new Bush-Rice dominance over foreign policy resulted simply in inaction: Cheney would recommend hawkish measures that Bush decided not to pursue. In the spring of 2007, Israeli officials brought the Bush administration intelligence showing that, with help from North Korea, Syria was secretly building a nuclear reactor. U.S. intelligence agencies subsequently confirmed the report. Israel wanted the United States to bomb the reactor. Cheney argued repeatedly that the United States should take military action to destroy the facility. Rice and Gates both strenuously registered their opposition. They were concerned that any American bombing could spark a wider regional war and perhaps lead to Syrian retaliation against American troops in Iraq. Bush agreed with these arguments, adding that he also did not like the implications of a surprise attack (which, referring to Pearl Harbor, Bush called the "Tojo option"). He rejected Israel's request for an American strike. Instead, on September 6, 2007, Israel bombed the facility on its own and succeeded in destroying it without a Syrian response. Bush later acknowledged he was not unhappy with the result.

The Middle East was the subject of several other internal disputes between Cheney and Rice, with Bush ultimately taking Rice's position. When Hezbollah carried out raids across Israel's border in the summer of 2006 and Israel retaliated by launching a war into Lebanon against Hezbollah, Bush (and other Western leaders) at first supported Israel's action as a legitimate response. After a week, other governments began to call for a cease-fire, but Bush refused to join, seeking to give Israel more time to weaken Hezbollah. Finally, in the third week, after Israeli bombers hit an apartment complex and killed twenty-eight civilians, Bush called in his advisers to talk about a cease-fire resolution. Cheney argued against it. "We need to let the Israelis finish off Hezbollah," he told Bush. "If you do that, America will be dead in the Middle East," Rice retorted. Bush came down on Rice's side and pushed successfully for a cease-fire.

In early 2007 Rice announced that the Bush administration would be willing to talk with the governments of Syria and Iran concerning the future of Iraq. Little came of this initiative, but the very willingness to launch the diplomacy underscored how Bush's foreign policy had changed; earlier, the administration's policy had been to isolate these two regimes.

. . .

The bitterest and most protracted of all the foreign-policy battles in Bush's second term involved North Korea's nuclear weapons program. North Korea was a particularly awkward subject for Bush. He had dispatched American troops into Iraq for the stated purpose of preventing it from developing nuclear weapons. North Korea's nuclear program was far more advanced than Iraq's—it had already produced enough material to make a bomb and was continuing to expand the program—yet the United States was raising few alarms and was doing little substantively to reverse the situation. Any American military action could have provoked North

Korea to retaliate with an artillery attack that could have devastated the vibrant South Korean capital of Seoul.

Bush had originally hoped that North Korea might follow the example of Libya. In 2003, after the invasion of Iraq, Libyan dictator Muammar Gadhafi, perhaps shaken by the American show of force, agreed to give up his nuclear weapons program in exchange for an end to the Western policy of isolating his regime. Bush sought to persuade North Korea and Iran to relinquish their nuclear programs as Libya had, in exchange for a new relationship with the United States. It turned out that neither government was willing to do so.

The situation reached a crisis in October 2006, when North Korea conducted its first nuclear test, thus becoming the world's ninth nuclear-weapons state. In response, Rice, with Bush's support, launched a series of diplomatic initiatives aimed at persuading North Korean leader Kim Jong Il to freeze and abandon his nuclear program. Over the following two years, Rice and her lead negotiator, Assistant Secretary of State Christopher Hill, offered North Korea a series of incentives to disarm, including oil supplies and removal from the State Department's terrorist list as well as the prospect of a nonadversarial relationship with the United States. North Korea proved willing to enter into an agreement that seemed to be the first step toward giving up its nuclear program but then repeatedly backtracked, sometimes after already accepting some of the benefits (such as the oil) that it had been offered.

These overtures were carried out over the bitter opposition of Cheney and other hawks in the administration. "Hill and Rice made concession after concession to the North Koreans," Cheney later wrote. "I concluded that our diplomats had become so seized with cutting a deal, any deal, with the North Koreans that they had lost sight of the real objective, which was forcing the North to give up its weapons."

Bush allowed Rice to proceed with her North Korean diplomacy until the last weeks of his administration, when the negotiations collapsed. After the United States removed Pyongyang from the State Department list of state sponsors of terror, North Korean officials refused to provide verification, such as soil and air samples, to prove it had halted its nuclear program. In 2009, after North Korea conducted another nuclear test, the Obama administration soon came to essentially the same conclusion Cheney had reached earlier: that North Korea's leaders did not view its nuclear program as a bargaining chip. They would not give up their nuclear weapons in exchange for other benefits, because they viewed nuclear weapons as essential to the survival of the regime.

With Iran, Bush went through a comparable evolution. After seeking throughout most of his presidency to isolate Iran, he sought negotiations to test whether Iran would abandon its nuclear program. Once again, Rice took the leading role. In 2007, she took part in a conference with an Iranian official but did not actually meet with him. The administration continued to hold to the long-standing U.S. government position that it would not talk directly with Iran until it complied with United Nations resolutions calling on it to stop enriching uranium. In the summer of 2008, Bush eased the policy, and Rice dispatched Undersecretary of State William Burns to meet with Iranian officials in Geneva. Conservatives were outraged. "Just when the administration has no more U-turns to pull, it does another," asserted John Bolton, Bush's former ambassador to the United Nations. Once again, as with North Korea, the talks produced no significant results, but they demonstrated how much Bush's foreign policy shifted in his later years in the White House.

Bush's efforts to stop the North Korean and Iranian nuclear programs were unsuccessful, but they did leave one important legacy: a new, increasingly powerful set of financial sanctions. In 2004, Bush approved a reorganization in which the Treasury Department was given full status in the intelligence community, with full access to all available information about money flows throughout the world. The Treasury Department established a new unit, the Office of Terrorism and Financial Intelligence, which soon focused its attention on North Korea. Treasury officials traveled widely in Europe and Asia to show international banks how they were unwittingly being used to facilitate illegal activity, such as counterfeiting, terrorism, or weapons programs. International banks were warned that if they continued to do business with one North Korean bank in Macao, they could be barred from doing business in the United States.

This approach proved surprisingly effective in freezing North Korea's ability to conduct international financial transactions, and before long U.S. officials began to impose financial sanctions on Iran in the same way, again with greater and greater success. After Bush left office, the Obama administration persuaded the Treasury Department official who had devised the new sanctions, a conservative Republican named Stuart Levey, to stay on the job. Over the following years, Obama came to rely on these international financial sanctions as his principal tool to push Iran into negotiations over giving up its program to enrich uranium. Although Cheney had proposed military action to stop Iran's nuclear program, Bush, with the support of Rice and Gates, chose diplomacy and financial sanctions instead.

• • •

The changes in the second term also included a new, intermittent emphasis on promoting democracy overseas. This policy focus came directly from Bush. The invasion of Iraq had failed to find evidence of a nuclear program, and by the beginning of his second term, as the war simmered on, Bush had elevated democracy into the principal rationale not just for the war itself but for his overall foreign policy. The prominent cold war historian John Lewis Gaddis had suggested that Bush include a line in his second inaugural address dedicating U.S. foreign policy to the goal of "ending tyranny in our world." Bush liked the idea, and he and his advisers began to speak in broad terms about the administration's "freedom agenda."

For a time, during the first eighteen months of the second term, it seemed as though Bush would be willing to press the cause of democracy in the Middle East, where the United States had long supported authoritarian regimes. He and his administration drew encouragement from a series of events in early 2005. In Iraq, citizens turned out to vote in large numbers, defying intimidation and proudly displaying the purple thumbs that showed they had cast their ballots. In Lebanon's Cedar Revolution, large-scale demonstrations had forced Syria to withdraw the troops that had been occupying the country. Optimists talked buoyantly of the "Arab spring" of 2005, a phrase that would soon be forgotten and then revived six years later.

That summer, Bush and Rice advocated for democracy with a dictator with whom the United States had deep and long-standing ties: Hosni Mubarak of Egypt. "A democratic Egypt would change the region like nothing else," Rice believed. In a one-on-one session with the Egyptian leader, she pleaded with him to give way for gradual democratic change. Mubarak told her that Egyptians do not like to be told what to do.

Undaunted, Rice gave a speech at the American University in Cairo, declaring that the United States was changing course in the Middle East and was "supporting the democratic aspirations of all people." The speech attracted considerable attention, and for a few months it seemed as though Mubarak was open to some limited political liberalization. These hopes were soon dashed. In parliamentary elections later that year, there were accusations that Egyptian security forces had sent out thugs to intimidate voters, and in 2006 Mubarak announced that he would keep in place the decades-old "emergency law" limiting free speech and assembly. Years later, Rice admitted to wondering whether her speech had "promised more rapid change than anyone could deliver, most especially the United States."

The idea of promoting democracy in the Middle East suffered a second setback in early 2006, when Palestinian legislative elections resulted in an unexpected victory for Hamas over the Fatah party of Palestinian Authority president Mahmoud Abbas. Through its military wing, Hamas had carried out a series of rocket attacks and suicide bombings against Israeli civilians, and it was on the State Department's list of terrorist organizations.

Before the vote, Israeli officials had voiced alarm about a Hamas victory, and the State Department had given some thought to urging that the vote be postponed. Bush rejected this approach. "America could not be in the position of endorsing elections only when we liked the projected outcome," he later explained. Afterward, recognizing that the election had been free and fair, Bush accepted the results and did nothing to prevent the Hamas victors from taking office. But the United States, European governments, and the United Nations soon joined together to make future aid conditional on Hamas's willingness to renounce violence. When Hamas refused to do so, its aid was cut off.

From then on, Bush's eagerness to promote the "freedom agenda" in the Middle East began to flag. In 2008, when Bush was scheduled to give a speech in Egypt on the importance of democratic change, aides drafted language in which he would draw attention to the case of Ayman Nour, a leading opposition figure jailed by Mubarak. Bush, however, ordered the speech rewritten and the reference to Nour taken out, because he did not want to offend Mubarak. Bush did open the way for new American funding in Egypt for the promotion of democracy and civil society, despite Mubarak's evident distaste for the programs.

Bush's second-term interest in democracy was reflected in more indirect ways and in regions outside the Middle East. One of his most significant and little-noticed diplomatic achievements was in forging a close, strong American relationship with India, the world's most populous democracy. India and the United States had remained at odds with one another for more than a half century amid a series of disputes over India's ties to the Soviet Union in the cold war, over U.S. support for Pakistan, and over India's development of nuclear weapons. In his second term, Bush proceeded to change the status quo. He negotiated a far-reaching nuclear agreement with India under which India agreed to put its nuclear reactors under international safeguards, while the United States opened the way for transfers of civilian nuclear equipment and other technology previously denied to India. The deal took four years to negotiate and implement and became the centerpiece of a new strategic relationship. Despite his low standing elsewhere in the world, in India Bush became the most popular American president since John F. Kennedy.

Laura Bush, meanwhile, embraced the cause of democracy in Burma, where the military junta had for years repressed dissent and had kept the Nobel Peace Prize winner Aung San Suu Kyi, whose party had won nationwide elections in 1990, under house arrest. In 2006, the first lady launched a public campaign for political change in Burma, writing op-ed pieces, convening conferences, appearing in the White House briefing room to criticize the junta, and eventually visiting a Burmese refugee camp in Thailand. "I wanted the people inside Burma to know that we heard them, and the junta to know it, too," she asserted.

Nevertheless, in Asia as in the Middle East, Bush applied his "freedom agenda" selectively and within careful limits. He maintained correct and cautious relations with China's Communist Party leadership, downplaying the issue of democratic change in the world's most populous nation. At one point in the fall of 2007, Bush took the unprecedented step of appearing in public with the Dalai Lama, awarding him the Congressional Gold Medal at an event in the Capitol Rotunda, to China's considerable displeasure. Yet Bush did this as part of an implicit trade-off: China had been pressing for Bush to attend the 2008 Olympics in Beijing, and Bush announced his agreement to go during the same general time period as the ceremonies for the Dalai Lama. In the end, China was too big for his freedom agenda.

• • •

At the end of 2006, after replacing Rumsfeld, Bush imposed a wholesale change in military strategy for Iraq that managed to reverse the downward course of the war there. After months of internal deliberation, he approved both a short-term increase in American troops in Iraq, commonly known as the "surge," and a shift from conventional military operations to a new emphasis on counterinsurgency. Bush later wrote that it was "the toughest and most unpopular decision of my presidency," a remarkable assertion, considering that he had also made the decision to launch the war in the first place.

It is difficult to exaggerate how much risk Bush took in ordering the surge. The war had been spiraling steadily downward, turning into a civil war between Sunnis and Shiites, and there was considerable domestic political momentum building for an American withdrawal. In pressing for the surge in troops, he overrode the resistance not merely of the Democrats in Congress, who had just regained the majority, and of an American public that was tired of the war, but also of senior military leaders and even his closest foreign-policy adviser, Secretary of State Rice.

Bush's decision was the culmination of several reviews of Iraq policy throughout the summer and fall of 2006. One took place informally within the military, where a rump group of officers began to question America's strategy in prosecuting the war. Among the principal figures were General David Petraeus, who had developed and written a new manual on counterinsurgency for the army, and Petraeus's own powerful mentor, retired general Jack Keane.

To that point, America's military strategy in Iraq had been to wage large-scale, conventional military operations against insurgents from fixed U.S. bases and, gradually, to hand over more and more of these operations to Iraqi forces. Rumsfeld had regularly used the metaphor that the United States needed to learn how to take its hand off the bicycle seat. The proponents of counterinsurgency argued that the conventional military approach created a distance between Americans and Iraqis; instead, they said, the U.S. troops should develop close ties with Iraqis at the local level, establish stability, and try to protect ordinary Iraqis from violence. Such a strategy, however, would require a large infusion of new American troops.

Another review of the military strategy was being carried out inside the White House itself. Throughout 2006, while insisting repeatedly in public that the war was going well in Iraq, Bush was secretly searching for a new approach. He asked his national security adviser, Steven Hadley, to seek out alternatives. Throughout the summer and fall, Hadley and his staff came to the conclusion that there would have to be more troops and a different strategy. These two inside and outside reevaluations of the conduct of the war were interrelated: Petraeus spoke almost daily with Meghan

O'Sullivan, an aide to Hadley who handled Iraq policy. All of these reevaluations were carried out surreptitiously, so as not to undermine the war efforts or the commanders in the field.

The only public reexamination of Iraq policy was carried out by a high-level commission called the Iraq Study Group, appointed by Congress in early 2006 to study the war and decide what should be done. By the fall, this panel of foreign-policy experts, headed by former secretary of state James Baker and former representative Lee Hamilton, was moving toward a recommendation to set a date for the withdrawal of American troops.

After appointing Gates as the new secretary of defense, Bush led a series of top-level meetings on Iraq. With even some Republican leaders urging troop withdrawals, it seemed as though the only options for Bush were either to continue the existing course or to begin to draw down U.S. forces. Nevertheless, with Bush's encouragement, Hadley and the NSC staffers laid out the arguments for sending more troops.

Military leaders were decidedly unenthusiastic. When Bush first presented the ideas for a surge to the Joint Chiefs of Staff at a Pentagon meeting, all of them "unloaded on him," according to Gates. They warned that a surge in troops to Iraq, requiring the extension of tours of duty in the war zone, would create too much strain on the army and might jeopardize its capabilities elsewhere around the world. The senior American commanders in charge of the war did not favor a surge, either. "I do not believe that more American troops right now is the solution to the problem," General John Abizaid, the chief of the Central Command, testified in Congress that November.

For her own part, Rice argued against inserting more American troops into what she termed blood feuds among the Iraqis. At one point, with other officials looking on, Bush rebuked her. "So what's your plan, Condi?" Bush asked. "We'll just let them kill each other, and we'll stand by and pick up the pieces?"

In early December 2006, the Iraq Study Group issued its final report. It called the situation in Iraq "grave and deteriorating" and recommended that the United States withdraw its combat forces from Iraq by the first quarter of 2008. However, the report included a sentence drafted by a leading Democrat on the panel, William Perry, formerly Bill Clinton's secretary of defense, which said that the commission could support "a short-term redeployment or surge of American forces" to stabilize the situation in Iraq before the withdrawal. Those words provided Bush with important political cover for the surge.

In a meeting with his advisers just before the end of 2006, Bush decided to send five more brigades (more than twenty thousand soldiers) of U.S. combat forces to Iraq, with support troops bringing the additional deployment to nearly thirty thousand. In reaching his decision, he turned aside a recommendation from his own commanders in Iraq that he scale back to a "mini surge" of only two new brigades. Separately, to mollify the Joint Chiefs of Staff, Bush at the same time authorized something they had long sought: an increase in the overall size of the military.

Bush announced the surge in a speech on January 10, 2007. "It is clear to me that we need to change our strategy in Iraq," he explained. He appointed Petraeus as the new commander of American forces in Iraq, a personnel change designed to carry out a new strategy of counterinsurgency. He also named a veteran diplomat, Ryan Crocker, as the new American ambassador to Iraq.

After three years of insisting that things were going well in Iraq, Bush finally admitted they were not. "The situation in Iraq is unacceptable to the American people—and it is unacceptable to me," he said in his speech. "Our troops in Iraq have fought bravely. . . . Where mistakes have been made, the responsibility lies with me."

• • •

Bush struggled on the home front to win enough public support for the surge to proceed. His standing in the polls had slipped so low that by December only 35 percent of Americans approved of his performance as president. With a new majority in both houses of Congress, the Democrats had the power to bring the Iraq War to an immediate close by cutting off funding for the war, if they were determined to do so.

For the Bush White House, this potential cutoff in money for the war was a serious concern. In the spring of 2007, Congress passed a funding bill for Iraq that included a timetable for the withdrawal of forces. Bush vetoed the bill, but he was then forced to accept revised legislation that set a series of "benchmarks" for progress in Iraq. As part of its oversight, Congress required that Petraeus and Crocker come home to report to Congress in September on the situation in Iraq.

By the summer of 2007, even Senate Republican leaders seemed to be wavering. Bush was so anxious about a loss of congressional support that he ordered his senior foreign-policy aides to hold off on travel. "I want everyone to stay home and fight the fight here," he told Rice. "I need you and Bob Gates meeting with Congress, meeting with the press—I need you out there defending the policy and buying time."

The September congressional hearings turned into a showdown over the surge and the war itself. Just before they started, Bush received a bit of unintentional help from some critics of the war. The antiwar group MoveOn published an advertisement in the *New York Times* that questioned Petraeus's patriotism. The ad referred to him as "General Betray-Us." It said he was "cooking the books" for the Bush White House, supposedly concealing information that the surge in Iraq had failed. The effect was to produce a wave of sympathy for the general; the ad alienated moderate Republicans and placed Democrats on the defensive as they sought to distance themselves from the MoveOn attack.

In two days of hearings, Petraeus and Crocker offered low-key testimony in which they contended that the surge was beginning to work. Casualty figures had increased when the surge started in early 2007, as the additional American troops entered the fighting, but by the summer they had begun to drop. Petraeus testified that the security situation was improving sufficiently that by mid-2008 he thought combat forces could be cut back to their pre-surge level. Senators Joe Biden, Barack Obama, and Hillary Clinton—all members of the Foreign Relations Committee who were running for the Democratic presidential nomination—questioned various aspects of Petraeus's testimony. At one point, Clinton told the general that his reports "really require the willing suspension of disbelief."

Yet neither they nor other Democratic leaders were willing to take on the responsibility for cutting off the money for the war, particularly at a time when a new strategy and new leadership had brought the first signs of progress. Bush had won this political battle: the Petraeus-and-Crocker hearings marked the end of any serious congressional effort to defund the war. After the hearings ended, Bush gave a televised speech promising that, over time, the American forces would scale back and shift the combat operations to Iraqi forces. For their part, the Democrats increasingly turned their attention away from Congress and toward winning the next presidential election.

In the summer of 2008, the surge ended, as Bush withdrew the last of the five additional combat brigades he had sent to Iraq. Its impact on the course of the war had been striking. There had been 112 American fatalities in the month of December 2006, when Bush decided on the surge, and 126 the following May, after the surge had increased the fighting. But then the figures dropped steadily and dramatically to the point where, in July 2008, there were just 13 American fatalities, the fewest since the start of the war in March 2003. Over that same time period from the end of 2006 to mid-2008, Iraqi civilian deaths dropped from 1,629 per month to 321.

· · ·

During his final year in office, Bush negotiated with the Iraqi prime minister Nouri al-Maliki two written agreements that paved the way for the United States to remain in Iraq for a time but also set a deadline for removal of all American forces by the end of 2011. Bush accepted this deadline reluctantly. In the past, whenever the Democrats in Congress had proposed a fixed timetable for withdrawal of troops from Iraq he had objected strongly. This time he persuaded himself that a deadline was acceptable, because if conditions changed the Iraqis could always amend the agreement and ask the Americans to stay there. In 2011, the Obama administration sought an extension of the agreement to permit a small-scale American presence, but Maliki and the Iraqis objected. As a result, U.S. troops left Iraq according to the timetable Bush had negotiated just before leaving office.

Ironically, during the 2008 presidential campaign, Barack Obama and his aides occasionally pointed to the actions of George W. Bush to make their case against John McCain, their Republican opponent. McCain was running as a hawk on foreign policy; he opposed fixing a time for removing American forces from Iraq, and he also criticized strongly the idea of negotiating with Iran. The Obama forces portrayed McCain as more conservative than Bush, because Bush set a deadline for withdrawal in Iraq and launched diplomatic initiatives with Iran and North Korea.

After Obama took office, critics on the left complained that his foreign policy sometimes appeared to be more a continuation of the Bush administration than a repudiation of it. Aides to Obama responded that if so, they were an extension of Bush's last years in the White House, not his early years. They drew the distinction between Bush's second term and his first.

It was a valid point. During his second term, Bush did operate differently. He moved increasingly away from his earlier reliance on Cheney, with his penchant for military power and unilateralism. Instead, Bush gave much greater leeway for Rice to pursue diplomatic initiatives that Cheney opposed. Yet Bush did not rely entirely on Rice, either. When she opposed the surge in Iraq, Bush went ahead anyway, choosing an unconventional strategy of counterinsurgency that even his own top military leaders had opposed.

When Bush took office in 2001, he had been far too willing to accept the advice of others. In his final years, he had become what he should have been earlier: a hands-on president willing to question what others told him and to become personally involved in both strategy questions and policy details.

None of this undid the damage he had caused by the military intervention in Iraq. One final episode before Bush left office embodied all the passions and tumult the war had engendered. In December 2008, Bush made a last visit to Iraq to sign the agreements he had negotiated with Maliki. During his final press conference there, an Iraqi journalist suddenly threw one of his shoes at Bush, and then the other. After artfully dodging the shoes, Bush made light of the incident. "If you want the facts, it's a size-ten shoe that he threw," he told reporters.

8

"I'm Going to Be Roosevelt, Not Hoover"

By the final year of his presidency, George W. Bush's life in the White House had settled into a series of daily routines. He brought his senior cabinet aides into the Oval Office to give him updates on the economy and on the war in Iraq, talking to them over his regular breakfast of cereal and fruit, or during a quick routine lunch of carrots, a chopped apple, and a hot dog.

A new presidential campaign was under way, but Bush was not involved. His party's candidate, John McCain, was keeping his distance; Bush was simply too unpopular to help him. The McCain campaign arranged for Bush to appear before the Republican National Convention by video rather than in person. Throughout that summer, Bush stayed in the background; his principal public event was to visit Beijing for the 2008 Summer Olympics. He did not believe his final months in office would be particularly eventful, either. "As September opened, we expected a harsh presidential campaign but an otherwise calm fall," wrote Laura Bush.

Those hopes were soon shattered. Between Labor Day of 2008 and Inauguration Day in January 2009, the American economy went through the most wrenching series of upheavals since the Great Depression. The Bush administration suddenly found itself lurching from one daily crisis to the next as the financial system froze up; America's leading banks tottered; its auto industry neared collapse; and its largest insurance company had to be rescued by the government. In the fourth quarter of 2008, the American economy declined at an annualized rate of 8.9 percent, and 651,000 Americans lost their jobs.

Bush's approach to the financial crisis stood in pronounced contrast to the way he had run the economy in the first years of his presidency. In 2001, he had been the driving force on behalf of his own policies, barnstorming around the country and seizing the airwaves to win congressional support for his tax cuts. When his first treasury secretary, Paul O'Neill, had raised objections, Bush had marginalized him and then forced him out. Conversely, by 2008, Bush was reacting to events rather than making them happen. He allowed a different treasury secretary, Henry Paulson, to take charge of handling the response to the financial crisis, giving him extraordinary leeway and authority, while Bush largely confined himself to approving Paulson's recommendations. In his last year in office, Bush possessed little if any clout on Capitol Hill. Most notably, in the throes of the financial crisis, Congress voted down the Troubled Asset Relief Program, his administration's principal legislative response, with Bush's own Republican Party leading the opposition.

Nevertheless, the role Bush played during the financial crisis was crucial, in the sense that without strong action by his administration, the banking and credit upheavals and ensuing recession could well have been far worse than they were. In approving strong governmental intervention, including massive bailouts of some of America's leading companies, Bush had to overcome his own conservative instincts and free-market principles. Simply put, he was determined to be on the right side of history. "If we're really looking at another Great Depression," he told his aides that fall, "you can be damn sure I'm going to be Roosevelt, not Hoover."

. . .

When it came to America's leading banks and securities firms, Bush saw himself as something of a populist, although his policies did not reflect that view. Paulson, who met with Bush often during the financial crisis, described the president's attitude toward Wall Street as a blend of "heart-of-the-country disdain" and "genuine contempt." Bush's grandfather had prospered on Wall Street, but both George H. W. Bush and George W. Bush had forsaken careers in finance for the oil industry. In the case of George W., his identity as a Texan ran deep, and with it came a skepticism toward Eastern elites, whether at Yale or on Wall Street.

Still, Bush did not give voice to these views during his two presidential campaigns as he raised unprecedented sums of money, with significant support from Wall Street. Bush's two tax cuts—especially the second, which cut levies on capital gains and dividends—benefited the financial industry more than any other sector of the economy, opening the way for those in the highest income brackets or with investment income to keep millions more each year.

In 2004, Bush nominated Alan Greenspan to a fifth term as chairman of the Federal Reserve, where for nearly two decades he had consistently opposed stronger regulatory control of financial markets. With Greenspan's term on the Fed set to expire in 2006, Bush appointed Ben Bernanke his successor, mostly because Bernanke was seen as likely to perpetuate existing policies. The following year, Bush appointed a new treasury secretary from the heart of Wall Street: Henry Paulson, the chief executive officer of Goldman Sachs. Paulson won from Bush a series of assurances that he would possess greater authority within the administration than had his predecessors. When he took the job, one newspaper profile predicted that with only two and a half years left in the administration, Paulson "may have little chance to make a mark on many economic issues."

· · ·

The blame for the financial crisis cannot be laid entirely at the doorstep of Bush or his administration. The policies that gave rise to the crisis had their origins well before he became president. There had been a trend toward deregulation of the financial system since the 1970s, and it had accelerated in the 1990s under the Clinton administration, with Treasury Secretaries Robert Rubin and Lawrence Summers playing leading roles alongside Greenspan. Together, they defeated an effort to regulate trading of financial instruments used to hedge risk, called derivatives, that were, a decade later, at the heart of the financial crisis. The Clinton administration also won passage of changes to the Glass-Steagall Act of 1933, so that, for the first time since the Great Depression, commercial banks could deal in securities transactions. Separately, Clinton also pushed to increase home ownership throughout the nation, with a special focus on lower-income families.

Bush did nothing to reverse any of these policies; instead, he further accelerated the trend toward deregulation and expanded home ownership. Opposition to "big government" and to government regulation were prominent themes in his campaigns, and as president his appointments to federal regulatory agencies such as the Securities and Exchange Commission and the Commodity Futures Trading Commission reflected these beliefs. He also gave further fuel to the boom in housing. If extending home ownership was for Clinton a means of helping minority groups and the poor, for Bush it became a component of his idea of an "ownership society," the slogan he used as part of his unsuccessful drive to privatize Social Security.

By Bush's second term, real estate brokers and originators were extending subprime mortgages to more and more buyers with a questionable ability to repay even the interest on the loans, let alone the principal. The mortgages were then sold to firms that "bundled" them together into packages of securities that were sold and resold in such a way that the weakness of the original mortgages was not apparent. There was little if any regulatory scrutiny of any of these transactions. The process was made all the more risky by the sale of derivatives and credit-default swaps, which amounted to large bets on the viability of these securities. Meanwhile, as the number of buyers for homes increased, housing prices spiraled ever higher. As they did, some home owners took out new home-equity loans based on the increased paper value of their houses.

Housing prices rose to the point where, by 2004, there was speculation about whether they represented a classic bubble. Greenspan dismissed the claims as "most unlikely" and continued to keep interest rates low. The following year he told the nation that while housing prices might not continue to increase, the market would simply "simmer down."

Soon after he was appointed treasury secretary, Paulson told Bush that the flood of unregulated capital into hedge funds, derivatives, and credit-default swaps "has allowed an enormous amount of leverage—and risk—to creep into the financial system." He warned that America's financial system had been suffering some major shock every four to eight years and that he was convinced another "disruption" was coming. By his own admission, however, Paulson had no idea when or how that disruption would come or how severe it would be. Significantly, he did not focus on housing or even mention the subject in his warning to Bush.

Housing prices peaked in late 2006, then leveled off and started to decline, leaving growing numbers of buyers "underwater" with homes worth less than the outstanding balance on their mortgages. Foreclosures steadily increased. In the spring of 2007, Paulson and Bernanke sought to dampen concern. Paulson told the public repeatedly that the problems that had been caused by subprime mortgages were "largely contained." He later acknowledged that he had failed to recognize how many bad mortgages had been written or how increasing amounts of leverage had amplified the negative consequences for the financial system of a housing decline.

The first tremors were felt in the summer of 2007, when the large French bank BNP Paribas stopped withdrawals from three hedge funds dealing in subprime mortgages. Although Bush announced a program to help home owners avoid foreclosures and the Federal Reserve cut interest rates, the economy slid downward toward recession. In early 2008, with Democratic support, Bush won passage of a onetime tax rebate aimed at stimulating the economy. At the time, Paulson and others thought the nation faced a short, V-shaped recession and would begin to turn upward by the middle of the year.

The falling home prices were causing the value of mortgage securities to drop rapidly, along with the stock prices of the banks that held them. In early March 2008, as Bush was preparing to give a

speech in New York the next day to reassure the markets, he and
Paulson argued over a few words in the draft. Paulson objected to
a line that said there would be no government bailouts. "We're not
going to do a bailout, are we?" Bush asked. Paulson told him the
financial system was so fragile that he wanted to leave the door
open for that possibility.

That same afternoon, Paulson learned that Bear Stearns, one of
Wall Street's most prominent investment banks, which had a large
exposure to mortgage securities, was on the brink of failure. In his
speech the following day, Bush avoided talking about bailouts, saying merely that the government needed to be careful about inter-
vening in markets. He was upbeat. "I'm coming to you as an
optimistic fellow. . . . Fortunately, we recognized the slowdown early
and took action," he said.

Paulson was concerned that Bear Stearns was so interconnected
to other investment banks and institutions, including large hedge
funds, that its failure would jeopardize some of them as well. Over
that weekend, with Bush's approval, he engineered a resolution
under which another bank, JPMorgan Chase, bought Bear Stearns
for a low share price while the Federal Reserve provided a $30 bil-
lion loan for a separate entity to buy Bear Stearns's worst mortgage
securities, thus effectively taking those more risky assets off
JPMorgan's hands.

Bush struggled to find a justification for this deal that would
be in accord with his long-stated opposition to government intervention in the economy. "You'll have to explain why it was necessary," he told his treasury secretary. Paulson repeatedly argued in
public that the failure of Bear Stearns would have been a disaster
because it was so interrelated with other financial firms. This
rationale, however, had an important consequence of its own: it
gave the impression that the Bush administration and the Federal
Reserve were unwilling to let a major financial institution go bankrupt. "After Bear Stearns, potential buyers of any failing financial
institution . . . would ask the Fed not whether it would lend, but
how much it was willing to kick in," wrote the financial journalist
David Wessel.

Over the following months, the stock prices of America's two leading institutions for housing finance, the Federal National Mortgage Association (Fannie Mae) and the Federal Home Loan Mortgage Corporation (Freddie Mac) tumbled downward as investors sold shares in fear that the companies would be brought down by their holdings of subprime mortgages. The two companies were privately owned but had been created and supported by the federal government; as a result, they were generally considered safe enough that foreign governments, including Japan, China, and Russia, held large stakes. In July, Paulson informed Bush that Fannie Mae and Freddie Mac were at risk, and he sought congressional approval to help rescue them, including the power to put taxpayer money into the institutions.

The housing institutions, which had their origins in the New Deal, had been a subject of recurrent Republican criticisms for decades. Bush himself had been calling for changes in Fannie Mae and Freddie Mac since 2003, making, by his own count, seventeen proposals for reform and for stronger regulation. Nevertheless, when faced with a potential collapse of Fannie Mae and Freddie Mac, Bush told Paulson that the first order of business was to "save their ass." By that point, foreign governments were weighing in with the administration to register concern about the safety of their bond holdings, and Bush wanted to stave off any action that could cause a decline in the dollar and damage to America's standing overseas. As a result, with Bush's approval, Paulson sought and obtained standby authority from Congress to put money into the firms and to seize control of them. In early September, the Bush administration put Fannie Mae and Freddie Mac into conservatorship, firing and replacing their top executives. The details were different, but once again the Bush administration had intervened to prevent financial firms from failing.

These actions were beginning to attract considerable criticism. On the political left, Bush and Paulson were accused of bailing out Wall Street, while on the right, critics complained that they were interfering in the markets. Just after the federal government took control of Fannie Mae and Freddie Mac, McCain and his running mate, Governor Sarah Palin of Alaska, wrote an opinion article for the *Wall Street Journal* under the headline "We'll Protect Taxpayers from More Bailouts."

Such criticism had an impact. By early September, Bush and Paulson were on the defensive about any further rescues of financial institutions. "All of us were well aware that after Fannie and Freddie, the country, Congress, and both parties were fed up with bailouts," Paulson wrote in his memoir.

That was the political climate as the financial crisis neared its apex. The week after the takeover of Fannie Mae and Freddie Mac, Bush and Paulson were informed that another Wall Street investment bank, Lehman Brothers, was on the brink of bankruptcy. Lehman, which was even larger than Bear Stearns, had run into liquidity problems stemming from its heavy purchases of mortgage securities, and its stock price was dropping rapidly.

This time, Paulson was determined to avoid using taxpayer money for another rescue. "I'm being called Mr. Bailout. I can't do it again," he told colleagues. With Bush's support, Paulson searched to find a last-minute buyer for Lehman Brothers, but other banks had little interest without the prospect of federal money to buy off the firm's toxic mortgage securities. For a time, Bush's hopes were focused on Barclays, the British bank, which seemed interested, but the chancellor of the exchequer threw cold water on the idea. The British did not want to import America's financial panic.

"What the hell is going on?" Bush asked Paulson. "I thought we were going to get a deal." But this time, there was no deal and no rescue. Bush and Paulson made the decision to let Lehman Brothers fail. On Monday, September 15, 2008, the firm declared bankruptcy.

· · ·

On the morning Lehman failed, Bush told Paulson he consoled himself that the bankruptcy would send the message that his administration was not going to keep bailing out failing companies. In short order, however, Bush would find himself unable to abide by this precept.

Paulson had believed that the consequences of a Lehman failure would not be so severe, because the near-bankruptcy of Bear Stearns six months earlier had put investors and other Wall Street firms on notice, giving them plenty of time to protect themselves from the collapse of a major company. This analysis turned out to be faulty: Bear Stearns had taught the opposite message, that the government would not allow a collapse.

After Lehman's bankruptcy, as Bush put it, "all hell broke loose." Credit immediately froze up as Wall Street firms refused to lend to one another or to Main Street businesses. Other major financial institutions were thrown into jeopardy as short-sellers drove stock prices down. On the day the bankruptcy was announced, the Dow Jones Industrial Average sank 500 points.

That same day, the ratings firms downgraded the debt for the mammoth insurance company American International Group (AIG), which had written large insurance contracts against defaults on risky mortgage securities. That action required AIG to put up more collateral to its lenders, and the firm, already in trouble, quickly veered toward bankruptcy. It was even more interconnected to financial institutions around the world than Bear Stearns or Lehman Brothers; the German and French finance ministers both urged the Bush administration not to let AIG go bankrupt. Moreover, AIG's failure would have affected municipalities and the life insurance, annuities, pension benefits, and retirement plans for ordinary Americans. Within forty-eight hours, with the Federal Reserve in the lead, the administration worked out the rescue of AIG, taking an 80 percent equity interest and effectively nationalizing it. Wielding the authority the government had just acquired, Paulson personally chose a new CEO for the company.

However reluctantly, Bush went along. Late in his presidency, he had become a hands-off president in dealing with economic policy, the opposite of his approach to foreign policy, where he had become increasingly a hands-on president. "If you are comfortable with this, then I am comfortable with it," he told Paulson and Bernanke. He thus found himself reversing after only two days the "no-more-bailouts" message he had hoped to send with the Lehman bankruptcy. By this juncture, he was irritated and baffled by what his economic advisers were telling him he needed to do. He questioned Paulson closely about why they could not let AIG fail without devastating the broader economy, wanting to know how the financial system had become so disastrously entangled.

The result of having to save AIG so soon after letting Lehman go down was to leave Bush without any guiding principles or rationale for his actions. His administration was against bailouts, until it was for them; it would rescue failing companies in some instances but not others. Investors and Wall Street were uncertain what to expect. Bush gave up on trying to be consistent. "Saving AIG would look like a glaring contradiction. But that was a hell of a lot better than a financial collapse," he later explained. These words epitomized his approach to everything else that happened in the following months. The only rationale that could serve to explain the administration's policies was one of necessity: Bush set principles aside and did whatever he had to do to keep the economy afloat.

Paulson launched a campaign to eradicate the word "bailout" from public discourse. He called the two rival presidential candidates, John McCain and Barack Obama, to urge them to refrain from calling the administration's action with respect to AIG a "bailout," maintaining that the word was a pejorative and inflamed public debate. Bush, too, sought to discourage the word, observing that the administration's actions did not seem like a bailout to the shareholders who lost most of their investments. Such arguments did not change the reality that for the larger purpose of rescuing the overall economy, the government was indeed committing taxpayers' money to save the companies, actions that fit the common meaning of "bailouts."

Over the following weeks, the Bush administration and the Federal Reserve took one unprecedented step after another. The Treasury Department used federal emergency money to guarantee money-market funds, so that they would not face a run on deposits and would be able to hold their net asset value of $1 a share. The Securities and Exchange Commission temporarily banned short-selling in nearly eight hundred financial stocks. Wall Street's

remaining investment banks were converted into bank holding companies, bringing them under the supervision and protection of the
Federal Reserve, whose strict rules would limit their ability to use
leverage to make risky investments.

All of these were measures the Bush administration was able to
take on its own, together with the Federal Reserve, which, though
independent, was coordinating its actions with Treasury. The most
significant, expensive government intervention, however, required
Bush to seek new legislation. Four days after the Lehman bankruptcy, Paulson announced that the Bush administration was
seeking money from Congress to buy up the toxic assets the banks
possessed stemming from mortgage securities.

This new program was called the Troubled Asset Relief Program, or TARP. Paulson had initially told Bush he needed at least
$500 billion, but Bush had asked, "Is that enough?" After realiz-
ing Congress would never approve $1 trillion, they somewhat arbi-
trarily settled on the final figure of $700 billion. It would be the
single biggest expenditure in the history of the federal government.

Bush launched a concentrated lobbying campaign to round up
the votes for TARP, with administration officials arguing that the
funds were needed to prevent a repeat of the Great Depression.
But the proposal proved extremely unpopular, and ten days after
it was unveiled the House of Representatives voted it down, 228
to 205.

In political terms, this first TARP vote was a bellwether. It dem-
onstrated how little influence Bush wielded near the end of his
presidency, particularly within his own party. Only sixty-five
Republicans, fewer than a third of the party's caucus in the House,
voted to support the president. Bush had not even managed to win
over a single Republican in the delegation from Texas, his home
state. The vote also represented the first demonstration of what
would later be called the Tea Party movement. On TARP, Republicans in Congress rejected the views of most of the business community as well as those of moderate Republican leaders and launched
out in the direction of a new form of economic populism.

However, it turned out that Congress could not live with the devastating impact of its own vote. Later that day, September 29, 2008, the Dow Jones Industrial Average dropped by 778 points, the largest one-day decline in its history. Bush and his advisers quickly decided to try again, and four days later the bill passed, 263 to 171. Even in this turnaround vote, the Republican rejection of Bush was clear: of the fifty-seven members of Congress who changed their votes from no to yes, thirty-three were Democrats.

• • •

In the midst of the financial upheavals, Obama and McCain were waging their general election campaigns to succeed Bush. The financial crisis and the two candidates' handling of it proved influential to the outcome. Paulson was briefing both candidates regularly; he found Obama to be thoughtful and supportive, while McCain worried him with populist-sounding rhetoric more attuned to the views of the Republican base.

At one critical juncture, McCain announced he was suspending his campaign and called for a bipartisan White House summit meeting to discuss the financial crisis. Administration officials were not enthusiastic about this idea, but Bush felt he couldn't say no to McCain. At the meeting the following day, Bush warned the participants of the need to act quickly, describing the situation in Texas vernacular: "If money isn't loosened up, this sucker could go down." Bush called on Obama, who calmly emphasized the gravity of the crisis and the need to get the TARP bill enacted. But when the president then asked for a Republican response from McCain, he declined to talk, saying he would pass until later. Eventually, he spoke briefly but said he was speaking only for himself rather than the party, evidently because of the intense divisions among the Republicans. Bush and Cheney were dumbfounded. Cheney, ordinarily no fan of Obama, later wrote that in that particular session the Democratic candidate was "very much at ease and in command of the situation," while McCain "added nothing of substance." The conference deteriorated into bickering between Republican and

Democratic leaders and resolved nothing. It ended when Bush finally stood up and declared, "Well, I've clearly lost control of this meeting. It's over."

For McCain, it was a disaster, and nothing he did in the following weeks could turn things around. On Election Day, Obama won with relative ease. American voters decided that after Bush, the next occupant of the White House should be a Democrat.

• • •

Bush was now reduced to the role of lame duck. Even so, the financial crisis meant that there was still quite a bit of history to be made, even in his final two months. In October, in a meeting at Camp David, French president Nicolas Sarkozy had asked Bush to convene a meeting of the United States, Britain, France, Germany, Italy, Canada, Japan, and Russia—the so-called G-8 nations, a well-established group whose roots dated back to the 1970s—to steer responses to the crisis. Bush spurned this idea and instead convened the first-ever summit of leaders of the so-called G-20, a larger group of economies that included China, India, Brazil, Mexico, Saudi Arabia, and South Korea. The groundbreaking session, held ten days after the American election, paved the way for seven further such summits over the following five years. The Obama administration would later portray Obama's emphasis on the G-20 as part of his effort to shift America's focus away from the old European powers and toward the rest of the world, but in fact it was Bush who took the first step.

During his final two months, Bush found himself approving several more rescues of leading American companies. In doing so, he vented his frustration. When told about Treasury Department plans to commit still more federal money to save AIG, Bush blurted out, "Are you asking me or telling me this is going to happen?" Paulson replied, "I'm telling you this is going to happen, Mr. President."

Once again, Bush was not going to interfere or to get involved in the details. Nevertheless, he continued to set the overall guidance. When told in mid-November that Citigroup was on the verge of failure and needed federal help, Bush at first voiced shock but eventually told Paulson, "Just don't let Citi fail."

In December, he took another far-reaching step by extending the series of bailouts from banking and financial institutions to the auto industry. Earlier that fall, car executives had informed Paulson they were facing bankruptcy, because their credit was drying up and suppliers were reluctant to keep doing business with them. A postelection effort to get help from Congress failed. Bush was faced with either opening the way for TARP funds for the car companies or allowing them to slide into bankruptcy in the weeks before he left office.

Prominent Republicans and conservatives, including Cheney, opposed any government intervention to rescue Detroit. Bush overrode their objections; he approved short-term loans from TARP funds of $13.4 billion for General Motors and $4 billion for Chrysler. One factor was his desire to avoid leaving Obama with an even more desperate economic situation than he would already face. The other was Bush's larger, continuing desire to avoid being remembered as another Herbert Hoover. "I had to safeguard American workers and families from a widespread collapse," he wrote. Any semblance of a commitment to laissez-faire economic policies, which Bush had proclaimed throughout his career, was gone after the auto bailouts.

• • •

There was one last piece of unresolved business, and it consumed Bush's final days as president. Like many of his predecessors, he was besieged by requests from individuals seeking presidential pardons for their crimes. Bill Clinton's last days in the presidency had been besmirched by his granting of a wave of pardons to friends, campaign donors, political figures, and even his half brother. Bush's father had granted six former senior officials pardons for their roles in the Iran-Contra affair.

For George W. Bush, the debate over last-minute pardons boiled down to a single individual: Scooter Libby, Cheney's former chief of staff. Libby had been convicted in 2007 on charges of perjury and obstruction of justice and had been sentenced to thirty months in prison. Bush had commuted the prison sentence a few months later. However, throughout Bush's final weeks in office, Cheney repeatedly pressed hard for a full presidential pardon for Libby.

Bush agonized. The president who called himself "the decider," suggesting he made choices easily, spent the final weekend of his presidency at Camp David agonizing over what to do about Libby. "Just make up your mind," Laura Bush told him. "You're ruining this for everyone." Finally, he decided to leave the jury's verdict on Libby in effect. When he told the vice president there would be no pardon, Cheney was infuriated, telling Bush he was "leaving a good man wounded on the field of battle." Even years later, Cheney would complain that Bush had lacked courage in failing to pardon Libby.

• • •

On January 20, 2009, George W. Bush spent his final hours as president in an America he never could have envisioned eight years earlier. Overseas, the United States was engaged in two wars. At home, despite the flurry of rescue efforts over the previous four months, the economy was still on the verge of collapse; in merely the single week before Bush left office, 524,000 more Americans signed up for unemployment benefits. Even the inauguration ceremonies that marked his final moments in office included a reminder of the upheavals of his tenure: Bush's aides had to warn the Obama team about reports of a terrorist attack on the event (which never materialized).

After Obama was sworn in, Bush, joined by friends and family, left Washington and flew home to Texas, the place with which he had always identified and where he always felt most comfortable. His trouble-filled presidency was over.

Epilogue

Of the ex-presidents in the modern era, George W. Bush was among the most private. He did not seek to insert himself into international diplomacy, like Jimmy Carter, nor to speak out on a range of issues, like Bill Clinton. He did not seek to rehabilitate his image by casting himself as an elder statesman, in the fashion of Richard Nixon.

While maintaining their ranch in Crawford, he and Laura settled into a new home they purchased in a wealthy neighborhood in North Dallas. In the early years after the White House, he preoccupied himself with the two basic tasks that all former presidents confront: his memoir and his presidential library. The memoir, *Decision Points*, was published in 2010, at a time when American troops were still in Iraq and the debates over Bush's counterterrorism measures were still raging. The book rekindled much of the rancor of the Bush presidency. Bush offered some admissions of error—his "bring 'em on" rhetoric and his handling of Katrina, for example—but also many defenses of his policies, enough to bring forth a wave of angry rebuttals. (The book found an audience, too, as it reached the top of the bestseller list and sold more than 2 million copies.)

In contrast, the ceremonies in 2013 to open the George W. Bush Presidential Library and Museum seemed to generate a certain mellowing in attitudes toward Bush, as various dignitaries tiptoed over the controversial aspects of his presidency in order to praise his personal qualities. "To know the man is to like the man, because he's comfortable in his own skin. He knows who he is. He doesn't put on any pretense," said President Barack Obama at the library opening. "He doesn't take himself too seriously. He is a good man." The Bush library, located at Southern Methodist University in Dallas, contained one feature unique for presidential libraries: an exhibit in which visitors are shown the key issues Bush faced and the often-conflicting views of his advisers. Visitors are then asked to choose which option they would take. Thus, the Bush presidency was transformed from "I'm the decider" to "You decide."

Bush traveled widely. He and his wife continued to visit Africa on behalf of PEPFAR, the program he established to combat AIDS. Indeed, that program emerged as the most universally admired aspect of the Bush legacy. At the library ceremonies, Bill Clinton thanked Bush for PEPFAR and asserted that "millions of people" are alive today because of the program, adding mordantly, "No president of my party could have passed that through the Congress." The singer-turned-activist Bono, who was instrumental in persuading the Bush administration to launch the program, had once teased Bush that as a result of PEPFAR the U.S. government had become the world's largest purchaser of condoms. Bush laughed; he later recorded the conversation in *Decision Points*. Still, there were places and events overseas that Bush avoided for political reasons: in 2011, he canceled what would have been his first postpresidential trip to Europe, a speech in Geneva, because human rights groups planned major demonstrations and said they would try to arrest him.

Before leaving the White House, Bush had told one interviewer that when he stepped down he planned to make money to "replenish the ol' coffers." He went at that task determinedly, following Clinton's example, by amassing millions of dollars through speaking appearances. With the help of a speakers bureau, he offered his services at $150,000. He often spoke to banks, hedge funds, trade groups, and similar private audiences, on occasion appearing together with Clinton. By mid-2011, two and a half years after leaving office, Bush's spokesman said he had delivered 140 paid talks, earning fees of at least $15 million.

In these speeches and other public appearances, however, Bush generally tried to avoid commenting on the issues of the day. Former vice president Dick Cheney emerged as the principal defender of the Bush administration's policies and as the leading critic of the Obama administration. Bush sought to avoid that role. "I think it's bad for the country to have former presidents out there undermining the current president," Bush explained. With a few exceptions, he refrained from public debate. One exception was the topic of immigration reform. Bush had consistently been pro-immigration throughout his career, and he remained outspokenly so after leaving the White House. He supported efforts in Congress to reform the immigration system, noting with regret that he had been unable to win passage of such legislation during his presidency. The other exception was internationalism: although the former president offered few opinions about specific foreign-policy issues, he warned against any broader drift by the United States toward isolationism.

As usual, he devoted considerable time to the affairs of the extended Bush family. His parents' health had begun to decline. He and his father were the first father-and-son pair of living ex-presidents in American history; John Adams had died while John Quincy Adams was still in the White House. The younger ex-president wrote an extended tribute to the older one: the book *41: A Portrait of My Father*, about the life and career of George H. W. Bush, was published in 2014. Meanwhile, the Bush clan was continuing to grow. In 2013, Bush became a grandfather when his daughter Jenna Bush Hager gave birth to a daughter, Mila.

In one bizarre episode, a computer expert based in Romania hacked into the email accounts of various members of the Bush family and began leaking them to American websites. The emails contained some prosaic exchanges among George W. Bush and his siblings, such as early planning for a funeral for their father, who was in poor health at the time. However, the hacked accounts contained one surprise revelation: in his postpresidential years, George W. Bush had taken up painting. The emails included photos Bush had mailed to his sister of some of his art. These included standard portraits of dogs and other animals but also other, unusual self-portraits that fit no conventional genre. One of them showed Bush's torso from the back as he stood in the shower, and another showed his feet as he lay in the bathtub. These quirky paintings, which had not been intended for public display, led to a wave of positive commentary. "OMG! Pigs fly. I like something about George W. Bush. A lot," wrote *New York* magazine's art critic Jerry Saltz. Bush acknowledged that he had been painting for as much as five to six hours a day, helped by an instructor who came to his home once a week.

The painting started when "he was desperate for a pastime," explained Laura Bush. "So John Lewis Gaddis, the historian from Yale, happened to be in Dallas, and they were talking. George said he was looking for a pastime now that he was home, and he said, 'Well, read [Winston] Churchill's book *Painting as a Pastime*.' So George did." George W. Bush told another interviewer: "Painting has changed my life in an unbelievably positive way." A year later, he put on exhibition in the Bush library a series of portraits of world leaders he had met, including Tony Blair, the Dalai Lama, Hamid Karzai, and Vladimir Putin.

Politically, Bush remained beyond the pale of respectability, even for Republicans, for years after leaving the White House. Always unpopular with the political left, he had also come to be spurned by the political right. Pointing to his extension of Medicare to cover prescription drugs and, especially, to the TARP program during the financial crisis, conservatives condemned Bush as a supporter of big government. At the Republican National Convention in 2012, Bush appeared only by video, as he had in 2008; the Republican nominee, Mitt Romney, was no more eager to be identified with Bush than John McCain had been four years earlier.

Since well before leaving the White House, Bush seemed to have yearned for a quiet existence as ex-president, one where he would no longer be in the spotlight. In 2006, as Bush was preparing to deliver his annual address to the U.N. General Assembly, he crossed paths with Bill Clinton in the lobby of the U.N. building. Afterward, Bush told one of his aides: "Six years from now, you're not going to see *me* hanging out in the lobby of the U.N."

. . .

In his memoir and in interviews after leaving the White House, Bush frequently maintained that any historical judgments about his presidency would be premature for decades. He recalled how Harry Truman's presidency and Gerald Ford's pardon of Richard Nixon came to be viewed more positively after the passage of time.

This argument that it will take a long time to judge Bush's actions may be valid for a few of the far-reaching measures Bush took. The counterterrorism measures Bush approved after September 11 fall into this category; years from now, historians will have greater perspective to evaluate whether or not they were necessary. The mere fact that Bush's successor, Barack Obama, a liberal Democrat, decided to continue some of these measures (such as the National Security Agency's surveillance activities) underscores the fact that Bush was not alone in deciding they were needed to help protect the United States against attack. A half century from now, if there are no further attacks on the American homeland comparable to al-Qaeda's attacks on the World Trade Center and the Pentagon, some future historians may conclude that Bush deserves credit. Contrarily, in a half century it may seem as if Bush's responses to September 11 were the starting point in the establishment of a surveillance state in which American rights to privacy were irretrievably damaged.

Yet there are other major aspects of the Bush presidency in which it does not seem too soon to draw conclusions. We can evaluate many of the actions of Bush and his administration against the predictions they made and the hopes they expressed at the time as well as the measurable consequences of those actions. Even judging by Bush's own standards, some of the most far-reaching and important initiatives of his presidency didn't work or turned out poorly.

At the top of the list is the war in Iraq. In both the buildup to the war and in the war itself, Bush and his top advisers misjudged badly what it would entail. They overestimated the international support the United States would be able to obtain for military action against Saddam Hussein. They asserted before the war that

American troops would need to stay in Iraq for no more than a couple of years; instead, the troops had to stay for more than eight years and then departed without having achieved the stability in Iraq that was envisioned. The Bush administration's public estimate before the war was that it would cost well below $100 billion; instead, it wound up costing $2 trillion, more than twenty times as much. The administration predicted that Americans would be greeted as liberators and thus failed to prepare adequately for the chaos that ensued. Administration officials believed Iraq might behave like Poland or Hungary after the collapse of Communism, when in fact the closer analogy from eastern Europe would have been the former Yugoslavia, which fell into bloody ethnic and religious conflict.

In the end, the military intervention in Iraq took the lives of more than 4,400 Americans. The war did succeed in toppling Saddam Hussein and ending the brutality of his regime, but the supposed weapons of mass destruction Bush administration officials told the country Saddam possessed were never found. The larger regional and international consequences of the intervention in Iraq also did not turn out as Bush and his administration had hoped. The war did not result in the spread of American influence in the Middle East; indeed, the practical, unintended consequence of the Iraq War was to leave Iran, America's principal adversary in the region, in a stronger position than before.

Intended originally as a short-term demonstration of American power and influence, the Iraq War over the longer term seemed to bring about the opposite. In its aftermath, America became increasingly cautious, more reluctant to become involved overseas. The broad strategic doctrine of unilateral preemption that Bush and Rice invoked before the war did not take root. Overall, the Iraq War now seems like a strategic blunder of epic proportions, among the most serious in modern American history, and it is difficult to see how future historians can decide otherwise.

So, too, it does not seem too soon to form judgments about the second most far-reaching aspect of Bush's legacy, his historic tax cuts. Bush argued that the tax cuts would stimulate the economy and spur economic growth; after a decade, these benefits seemed dubious at best. The harmful long-term consequences, however, were incalculable. The tax cuts ushered in a new era of massive budget deficits, as the federal government became increasingly short of revenues. Meanwhile, the tax cuts changed the very nature of American society, creating vastly greater disparities in income and assets between wealthy Americans and the middle classes, so that, more and more, they led different lives and had little in common with one another. Although Barack Obama eventually overturned the Bush tax cuts on upper-income Americans, that action did not reverse the enormous impact of what had already taken place: over a period of nearly a decade, enormous sums that would otherwise have been routinely taxed were instead left in the hands of the wealthy.

American presidents tend to be evaluated, above all, on how they perform in two areas: on issues of war and peace and on the economy. By this standard, Bush, who departed from the White House with America embroiled in two wars and the worst economic crisis since the Great Depression, is likely to rank low in the judgments of future historians.

To be sure, not all of this legacy was of Bush's creation. One of the two wars he left behind, in Afghanistan, began as a response to a direct attack on the United States. The financial crisis resulted from a wave of deregulation that dated back to the Clinton years or even earlier and that Bush further accelerated. Indeed, history may judge that, through actions such as the TARP program, Bush and Barack Obama together deserve credit for the fact that the financial crisis wasn't even worse. Nevertheless, major parts of the Bush legacy—the Iraq War, the tax cuts—were entirely of Bush's own choosing, and their impact was pervasive, affecting many of his other policies. The war in Iraq, for example, diverted attention and resources away from the war in Afghanistan, while the tax reductions strained resources both for the two wars and for other ventures abroad and at home.

Bush was not responsible for all of America's difficulties, yet the far-reaching actions he took, particularly on Iraq and the tax cuts, further compounded the nation's problems. Once, in the midst of a discussion with his military advisers, Bush made a telling observation. "Somebody has got to be risk-averse in this process, and it better be you, because I'm sure not," he said. George W. Bush was, for sure, not risk-averse. He took gambles both in foreign policy and with the economy. Sometimes, they paid off. Yet overall the country paid heavily for the risks he took.

Notes

PROLOGUE

1 only three trips outside the United States: See, for example, David
   A. Sanger, "Rivals Differ on U.S. Role in the World," *New York Times*,
   October 30, 2000; Warren Hoge, "Other Nations Regard Campaign
   with Interest and Wonder," *New York Times*, November 6, 2000;
   Thomas L. Friedman, "I Love D.C.," *New York Times*, November 7,
   2000.
1 "Laura and I went to see 'Cats'": Transcript, interview of George W.
   Bush by Sir David Frost of BBCTV, November 12, 2003.
2 "Try being a VPK": David Maraniss, "The Bush Bunch," *Washington Post Magazine*, January 22, 1989.
2 The survey found: Nicholas D. Kristof, "A Father's Footsteps Echo
   Throughout a Son's Career," *New York Times*, September 11, 2000.
3 "The one somewhat touchy area": Robert M. Gates, *Duty: Memoirs of
   a Secretary at War* (New York: Alfred A. Knopf, 2014), pp. 5–7, 95.

1: "A GOOD-TIME GUY"

5 castor oil . . . "spoiled little boy": Barbara Bush, *Barbara Bush: A
   Memoir* (New York: Charles Scribner's Sons, 1994), pp. 27–35.
6 "too young to know": Amy Cunningham interview with Barbara
   Bush, for "Goodbye to Robin," *Texas Monthly*, February 1988.
7 "Why didn't you tell me?": George Lardner Jr. and Lois Romano,
   "A Texas Childhood: A Sister Dies, a Family Moves On; Loss Creates Strong Bond Between Mother, Son," *Washington Post*, July 26,
   1999.
7 "saved my life": Cunningham interview with Barbara Bush.
7 "She kind of smothered me": Patricia Kilday Hart, "Don't Call Him
   Junior," *Texas Monthly*, August 1988.

7 "of Mother's personality": George W. Bush, *Decision Points* (New York: Crown, 2010), p. 7.

8 "hardest thing I did": Ibid., p. 11.

8 "a sense of frivolity": Bill Minutaglio, *First Son: George W. Bush and the Bush Family Dynasty* (New York: Three Rivers Press, 1999), p. 64.

8 "a little swagger": Ibid., p. 66.

9 "big man on campus": Lois Romano and George Lardner Jr., "Bush: So-So Student but a Campus Mover," *Washington Post*, July 27, 1999.

9 college board scores: Nicholas D. Kristof, "Earning A's in People Skills at Andover," *New York Times*, June 10, 2000.

9 back of the page: Bush, *Decision Points*, p. 13.

9 Red Sox star Carl Yastrzemski: Ibid., p. 15.

9 "a good-time guy": Romano and Lardner, "Bush: So-So Student."

9 its first toga party: Minutaglio, *First Son*, p. 95.

10 "only a cigarette burn": "Branding Rite Laid to Yale Fraternity," *New York Times*, November 9, 1967, obtained from Steven Weisman.

11 "a better man": "Born to Run," *Texas Monthly*, April 1994, cited in Minutaglio, *First Son*, p. 85.

11 "I want to give nothing," Romano and Lardner, "Bush: So-So Student."

11 opened the White House to his Yale classmates: Interview with Derek Shearer; Elisabeth Bumiller, "On Gay Marriage, Bush May Have Said All He's Going To," *New York Times*, March 1, 2004.

12 Dallas Cowboys: George Lardner Jr. and Lois Romano, "At Height of Vietnam, Bush Picks Guard," *Washington Post*, July 28, 1999.

13 more money for Houston's Ellington Air Force Base: Joe Hagan, "Truth or Consequences," *Texas Monthly*, May 2012.

14 accusations of favoritism always lingered: The Guard issue did, ironically, lead to the downfall of CBS anchorman Dan Rather, who in 2004 aired a report on Bush that was later found to have been based on a forged document. Hagan, "Truth or Consequences."

15 "You wanna go mano a mano right here?": Maraniss, "Bush Bunch."

15 "I was a boozy kid," Bush, *Decision Points*, p. 21.

15 the decade after college as a time to explore: Ibid., p. 16.

15 expeditions to the Hillbilly Ranch: Michael Kranish, "Hallmarks of Bush Style Were Seen at Harvard," *Boston Globe*, December 28, 1999.

16 "Today is George's twenty-ninth birthday": Jeffrey A. Engel, ed., *The China Diary of George H. W. Bush* (Princeton: Princeton University Press, 2008), p. 352.

17 "close to my mother on that day": George W. Bush, *A Charge to Keep* (New York: Harper Perennial, 2001), p. 175.

17 The campaign taught him an important lesson: Bush, *Decision Points*, p. 41.

18 the tennis star John Newcombe: Steve Lillebuen, "Newked: John Newcombe Breaks Silence on the Bender That Got George W. Bush Arrested," *Sydney Morning Herald*, October 10, 2014.

18   a sign that it was time for him to settle down: Ibid., p. 25.
18   miniature golf: Laura Bush, *Spoken from the Heart* (New York: Charles Scribner's Sons, 2010), pp. 94–96.
18   "ferociously tart-tongued": Ibid., pp. 124–25.
18   his uncle Jonathan Bush: Molly Ivins and Lou Dubose, "Slick W.," *Mother Jones*, March/April 2000.
19   "Please Lord": Laura Bush, *Spoken from the Heart*, p. 116.
19   $15,000 investment . . . $840,000: Ivins and Dubose, "Slick W."

2: THE RISING POLITICIAN

20   "an occasional bender": Bush, *Decision Points*, p. 33.
20   "he could be a bore,": Laura Bush, *Spoken from the Heart*, p. 118.
20   "what is sex like after fifty?": Bush, *Decision Points*, p. 33.
20   Broadmoor Hotel: Ibid., pp. 1–3.
21   go to heaven: Minutaglio, *First Son*, p. 289.
21   a gathering at Camp David: Ibid., p. 206.
21   her husband's decision to quit drinking: Laura Bush, *Spoken from the Heart*, p. 118.
21   "looked in the mirror": Minutaglio, *First Son*, p. 210.
22   "these fakes": Barbara Bush, *Barbara Bush: A Memoir*, p. 215.
22   a role within the Bush campaign: Minutaglio, *First Son*, p. 211.
22   A former Assembly of God minister: Robin Abcarian, "Behind the Secret Tapings of Bush, a Life Is Changed," *Los Angeles Times*, March 25, 2005; Minutaglio, *First Son*, pp. 212–13.
22   a rival Republican presidential candidate, Jack Kemp: Lois Romano and George Lardner Jr., "Bush's Move Up to the Majors," *Washington Post*, July 31, 1999.
22   "How do we know we can trust you?": Bush, *A Charge to Keep*, pp. 178–79.
23   "loyalty enforcer": Ibid., p. 180.
23   "Roman candle of the family": Richard Ben Cramer, *What It Takes: The Way to the White House* (New York: Random House, 1992), p. 17.
24   Scrub Team: Minutaglio, *First Son*, p. 232.
24   the ouster of John Sununu: James Gerstenzang, "Sununu Quits to Avoid Being Campaign Drag," *Los Angeles Times*, December 4, 1991.
24   the exclusive White House dinner: Barbara Bush, *Barbara Bush: A Memoir*, pp. 414, 460.
24   dump Vice President Dan Quayle: Bush, *Decision Points*, p. 49.
25   "Watching a good man lose,": Ibid., p. 50.
26   a wave of news stories and magazine profiles: See, for example, Hart, "Don't Call Him Junior"; Julie Morris, "Bush's Son Eyes Texas's Top Job," *USA Today*, May 31, 1989.
26   "a major commitment like that": Romano and Lardner, "Bush's Move Up to the Majors."

26 "our shaky pitching rotation": Bush, *Decision Points*, p. 46.

27 $14.9 million: Minutaglio, *First Son*, p. 322.

27 "older than his vice president": Roberto Suro, "One of Bush's Campaign Advisers Is Also His Son," *New York Times*, April 26, 1992.

27 "the talent that George Bush has": Romano and Lardner, "Bush's Move Up to the Majors."

28 "All that I ask": Skip Hollandsworth, "Born to Run," *Texas Monthly*, May 1994.

29 "heaven is only open": Ken Herman, "The Candidates and the Higher Authority," *Houston Post*, October 2, 1994.

29 "compassionate conservative": Minutaglio, *First Son*, pp. 214, 306.

29 "a lot of capital to spend": Sam Howe Verhovek, "Bush Stumbles on Taxes in Texas," *New York Times*, May 31, 1997.

30 "a fair shot at achieving their dreams": Lani Guanier, "An Equal Chance," *New York Times*, April 23, 1998.

31 "If you're Canadian": Patrick Beach, "The First Son: George W. Bush Had His Rebellions," *Austin American-Statesman*, June 13, 1999.

31 "It's a six-inch putt": Frank Bruni, *Ambling into History: The Unlikely Odyssey of George W. Bush* (New York: HarperCollins, 2002), p. 148.

31 Rove began talking to Bush: Karl Rove, *Courage and Consequence: My Life as a Conservative in the Fight* (New York: Threshold Editions, 2010), p. 112.

32 baby-boom generation: Bush, *Decision Points*, p. 49.

32 "our Clinton": Minutaglio, *First Son*, p. 305.

32 "plotting, planning and scheming,": Rove, *Courage and Consequence*, p. 114.

33 "The race is his to lose": John J. Miller and Ramesh Ponnuru, "Handicapping 2000," *National Review*, November 9, 1998.

33 52 percent: Dan Balz, "Starting Early and Urgently: Presidential Contenders Leave Calendar in Dust," *Washington Post*, April 4, 1999.

33 "The bottom line remains money": Kevin Merida, "A Campaign of Quitters Cites the Bush Factor," *Washington Post*, October 28, 1999.

33 "funny and irreverent": Condoleezza Rice, *No Higher Honor: A Memoir of My Years in Washington* (New York: Crown, 2011), p. 2.

35 Social Security trust fund: Jill Lawrence, "McCain Knocks Bush's Tax-Cut Proposal," *USA Today*, January 6, 2000.

35 "chose to sire children without marriage": Rove, *Courage and Consequence*, pp. 151–53.

35 "Don't give me that shit": James Carney, "Frenemies: The McCain-Bush Dance," *Time*, July 16, 2008.

36 "Grecians" . . . "put food on their family": Bruni, *Ambling into History*, p. 39.

36 "stow your expectations . . . Last chance for malaprops": Ibid., p. 5.

36 Rove resisted: Rove, *Courage and Consequence*, pp. 166–76; Bush, *Decision Points*, pp. 69–70.

37 "a great choice": Bush, *Decision Points*, p. 66.

37 "If we're an arrogant nation": Transcript of Second Bush-Gore Debate, Winston-Salem, NC, October 11, 2000.

38 "I occasionally drank too much": Rove, *Courage and Consequence*, p. 190.

38 a Bush friend phoned John Newcombe: Lillebuen, "Newked."

38 "It was jarring": Ibid., pp. 192–93.

38 at 7:49 p.m.: The times and election-night chronology are taken from Jeffrey Toobin, *Too Close to Call: The Thirty-Six-Day Battle to Decide the 2000 Election* (New York: Random House, 2001), pp. 17–25.

39 "Circumstances have changed . . . Are you saying?": Gore and Bush quotes from ibid., p. 25.

40 "And I promised him": Transcript of Gore concession speech, *New York Times*, December 14, 2000.

3: THE NEW PRESIDENT AND HIS TAX CUTS

42 "Civility is not a tactic or a sentiment": Transcript of George W. Bush First Inaugural Address, January 20, 2001.

43 fritter away the surplus: Alison Mitchell, "Bush Says That the Bottom Line on Gore's Proposals Would Consume the Surplus," *New York Times*, September 7, 2000.

44 "too much of the people's money": Bush, *Decision Points*, p. 442.

44 more than a third of all the tax savings: "The Real Tax Plan," *Washington Post*, February 11, 2001.

44 "I have about $125 billion of surplus": Ron Suskind, *The Price of Loyalty: George W. Bush, the White House, and the Education of Paul O'Neill* (New York: Simon & Schuster, 2004), p. 136.

45 "We'll be negotiating with ourselves": Jonathan Weisman, "Bush's Tax-Cut Hardball Seems to Have Paid Off," *USA Today*, May 29, 2001.

46 "The election of President Bush changed that dramatically": John Lancaster and Helen Dewar, "Jeffords Tips Senate Power," *Washington Post*, May 25, 2001.

46 "Reagan proved deficits don't matter": Suskind, *Price of Loyalty*, p. 291. In his memoir, Cheney elaborated: "Of course I thought deficits mattered. I just believed that it was important to see them in context." Reagan's deficits had helped to win the cold war, he maintained. See Dick Cheney, *In My Time* (New York: Threshold Editions, 2011), p. 136.

46 "Didn't we already give them a break at the top?": Suskind, *Price of Loyalty*, p. 299.

46 U.S. presidents have raised taxes: See, for example, Ronald Brownstein, "Bush Breaks with 140 Years of History in Plan for Wartime Tax Cut," *Los Angeles Times*, January 13, 2003.

46 more than $100 billion: Bob Davis, "Bush Economic Aide Says Cost of Iraq War May Top $100 Billion," *Wall Street Journal*, September 16, 2002.

47 Sales of $600-a-night luxury hotel suites: Jon E. Hilsenrath and Sholnn Freeman, "Affluent Advantage: So Far, Economic Recovery Tilts to Highest-Income Americans; They Gain More, Spend More," *Wall Street Journal*, July 20, 2004; Matt Stearns, "For the Richest Americans, the Economy's Fine," *Philadelphia Inquirer*, March 28, 2004.

47 Walton family: Calculations based on Wal-Mart corporate filings.

47 surplus of $86 billion . . . deficit was $642 billion: Data from Congressional Budget Office, 2010.

48 "incomplete state of scientific knowledge": Douglas Jehl and Andrew C. Revkin, "Bush, in Reversal, Won't Seek Cut in Emissions of Carbon Dioxide," *New York Times*, March 14, 2001.

49 Bush viewed this question: Bush, *Decision Points*, pp. 109–25.

49 One of the most prominent proponents was Nancy Reagan: Ibid., p. 106.

51 "Let's show them . . . important White House signings": Ibid., p. 275.

51 Bush and Kennedy stood side by side: Elisabeth Bumiller, "Focusing on Home Front, Bush Signs Education Bill," *New York Times*, January 9, 2002.

4: SEPTEMBER 11

53 "one of the finest foreign policy teams": James Mann, *Rise of the Vulcans: The History of Bush's War Cabinet* (New York: Viking, 2004), p. ix.

53 "retreads": Thomas L. Friedman, "The Way We Win," *New York Times*, November 14, 2000.

53 "George II was an obedient son": Maureen Dowd, "When the Boy King Ruled," *New York Times*, December 31, 2000.

54 "all right-wing nuts, like you,": Colin Powell, *My American Journey* (New York: Ballantine Books, 1995), p. 526.

54 Rumsfeld also developed an antipathy toward Rice: Donald Rumsfeld, *Known and Unknown* (New York: Sentinel, 2011), pp. 325–30.

54 Rice thought that Rumsfeld had trouble: Rice, *No Higher Honor*, p. 21.

55 Bush picked up the *Washington Post*: Bush, *Decision Points*, pp. 90–91; Rice, *No Higher Honor*, pp. 35–36.

55 "too far forward on your skis": Karen DeYoung, *Soldier: The Life of Colin Powell* (New York: Alfred A. Knopf, 2006), pp. 323–26.

55 "The President was really angry": Rice, *No Higher Honor*, pp. 41–44.

56 "We had to be able to build": Cheney, *In My Time*, p. 325.

57   "by far your biggest threat is Bin Laden": National Commission on
      Terrorist Attacks, *The 9/11 Commission Report* (New York: W. W.
      Norton, 2004), p. 199.

57   she was wary of him: Rice, *No Higher Honor*, p. 64.

57   "there was a loss of urgency": George Tenet, *At the Center of the Storm:
      My Years at the CIA* (New York: HarperCollins, 2007), p. 139.

57   Bush later maintained: *9/11 Commission Report*, pp. 260–62; Bush,
      Decision Points, p. 135.

58   Rice forwarded the decision to Bush: Rice, *No Higher Honor*, p. 70.

58   continuity-of-government exercises: Mann, *Rise of the Vulcans*, pp.
      138–49.

58   no record of such a conversation and reason to doubt: See Barton
      Gellman, *Angler: The Cheney Vice Presidency* (New York: Penguin
      Press, 2008), pp. 118–28.

59   "Mr. President, you cannot come back here": Rice, *No Higher Honor*,
      p. 73.

59   "Today, our nation saw evil": George W. Bush, "Address to the
      Nation on the September 11 Attacks," September 11, 2001.

59   "The rest of the world hears you": George W. Bush, "Remarks to
      New York Rescue Workers," September 14, 2001.

59   "until every terrorist group of global reach": George W. Bush,
      "Address to the Joint Session of the 107th Congress," September
      20, 2001.

59   "There's an old poster out West": George W. Bush remarks in visit
      to the Pentagon, September 17, 2001.

59   "a little too blunt": Bush, *Decision Points*, p. 140.

60   "began coming of age this weekend": R. W. Apple Jr., "President
      Seems to Gain Legitimacy," *New York Times*, September 16, 2001.

60   "as strong and forthright": "Mr. Bush's Most Important Speech,"
      New York Times, September 21, 2001.

60   "He's done a first-rate job": Mike Blanchard, "'Clear, Confident'
      Bush Rallies U.S.," *Ottawa Citizen*, September 24, 2001.

60   "We will make no distinction": George W. Bush, "Address to the
      Nation on the September 11 Attacks," September 11, 2001.

60   Bush and Rice had parsed the words. . . . Rice said it reflected: Rice,
      No Higher Honor, pp. 76–77.

60   "Iraq has to pay a price": Tenet, *At the Center of the Storm*, p. xix.

60   argued specifically for military action against Iraq: Rice, *No Higher
      Honor*, pp. 86–87.

61   "expensive weapons on sparsely populated camps": Bush, *Decision
      Points*, p. 191.

62   "dressed up with nowhere to go": Rice, *No Higher Honor*, p. 79.

62   "The mission must determine the coalition": Rumsfeld, *Known and
      Unknown*, p. 354.

62   "boots on the ground": Bush, *Decision Points*, p. 191.

63 "Either you are with us, or you are with the terrorists": George W. Bush address to Joint Session of Congress, September 20, 2001.

64 "I should have pushed Congress": Bush, *Decision Points*, p. 162.

65 The vice president was the driving force: Cheney, *In My Time*, p. 348, and Tenet, *At the Center of the Storm*, p. 237.

66 "I want a plan tomorrow. . . . They just need to move": Rice, *No Higher Honor*, pp. 94–96.

66 new system of tribunals: Gellman, *Angler*, pp. 162–68.

67 "The Vice President was, as I remember it, the one": Rice, *No Higher Honor*, p. 106.

67 no constitutional protections: Bush, *Decision Points*, p. 166.

68 "weasel out": Douglas J. Feith, *War and Decision: Inside the Pentagon at the Dawn of the War on Terrorism* (New York: HarperCollins, 2008), p. 161.

68 Powell asked for a National Security Council meeting: DeYoung, *Soldier*, p. 369.

68 In a written memo, Bush promised: Rice, *No Higher Honor*, p. 108.

69 black sites: Dana Priest, "CIA Holds Terror Suspects in Secret Prisons," *Washington Post*, November 2, 2005, and Jane Mayer, *The Dark Side: The Inside Story of How the War on Terror Turned into a War on American Ideals* (New York: Doubleday, 2008), pp. 139–81.

69 "renders obsolete Geneva's strict limitation": Mayer, *Dark Side*, p. 124.

69 its first high-level al-Qaeda operative: Bush, *Decision Points*, p. 168.

69 turned down two of the CIA's proposals: Gellman, *Angler*, p. 177; Bush, *Decision Points*, p. 169.

70 "Damn right": Bush, *Decision Points*, p. 170.

70 subjected to waterboarding 183 times: Scott Shane, "Waterboarding Used 266 Times on 2 Suspects," *New York Times*, April 20, 2009.

70 "proved difficult to break": Bush, *Decision Points*, p. 170.

70 "the most senior legal officers . . . Had I not authorized waterboarding": Ibid., pp. 169–71.

71 "I think there was a huge sense": Gates, *Duty*, p. 93.

5: IRAQ

72 "it does not end there": Bush address to Congress, September 20, 2001.

72 "phase one": Powell interview on NBC's *Meet the Press*, September 23, 2001.

72 placed Somalia under intense surveillance: Mann, *Rise of the Vulcans*, p. 309.

73 "axis of evil": George W. Bush, "State of the Union Address to the 107th Congress," January 29, 2002.

74 battle plans for an invasion of Iraq: Bush, *Decision Points*, p. 234.

74 following the model of . . . Harry S. Truman: Ibid., pp. 174–75.
75 "We must take the battle to the enemy": George W. Bush address, "West Point Commencement," June 1, 2002.
75 "will not hesitate to act alone": The National Security Strategy of the United States of America, September 2002, http://georgewbush-whitehouse.archives.gov/nsc/nss/2002/.
76 "Saddam is a familiar dictatorial aggressor": Brent Scowcroft, "Don't Attack Saddam," *Wall Street Journal*, August 15, 2002.
76 "Son, Brent is a friend": Bush, *Decision Points*, p. 238.
76 "You are doing the right thing": Ibid., p. 225.
76 "Take it to the U.N.": DeYoung, *Soldier*, pp. 401–2.
77 "Saddam has perfected the art of cheat and retreat": Vice President Dick Cheney speech to Veterans of Foreign Wars, August 26, 2002.
77 He ordered Rice to call Cheney: Rice, *No Higher Honor*, p. 180.
77 "Your man has got *cojones*": Bush, *Decision Points*, p. 239.
77 "time was of the essence": Peter Baker, "Rove's Version of 2002 War Vote Is Disputed," *Washington Post*, December 1, 2007.
77 Rove . . . had argued for a postelection vote: Rove, *Courage and Consequence*, pp. 300–302.
78 first president since Franklin Roosevelt: Ibid., p. 315.
80 "we settled on the one issue": Defense Department transcript of Wolfowitz interview with *Vanity Fair*, May 9, 2003.
80 "I doubt it was even the principal cause": Tenet, *At the Center of the Storm*, p. 321.
80 an Iraqi plot to kill his father: Michael Isikoff, "Saddam's Files," *Newsweek*, March 22, 2008, http://www.thedailybeast.com/newsweek/2008/03/22/saddam-s-files.html.
80 "You just keep on digging": Rice, *No Higher Honor*, p. 171.
81 vindicated in the case of Libya: Bush, *Decision Points*, pp. 267–68.
82 "pre-9/11 mindset": Cheney, *In My Time*, p. 388.
82 "we would have waited too long": Bush, *Decision Points*, p. 229.
82 "slam dunk" . . . to shift the blame to the CIA: Tenet, *At the Center of the Storm*, pp. 362–67.
83 Saddam told FBI debriefers: Bush, *Decision Points*, p. 269.
83 "It wasn't possible just to stand still": Rice, *No Higher Honor*, p. 201.
83 "This is something Condi has wanted": Ibid., p. 190.
85 "But the intelligence was wrong": Bush, *Decision Points*, p. 254.
85 "It was a big mistake": Ibid., pp. 256–57.
86 had surpassed $2 trillion: John Nagl, "What America Learned in Iraq," *New York Times*, March 20, 2013.
87 "I really do believe that we will be greeted as liberators": Cheney interview on NBC's *Meet the Press*, March 16, 2003.
87 "our nation building capabilities were limited": Bush, *Decision Points*, pp. 249–50.
87 He had relied on assurances from Rumsfeld: Ibid., pp. 258–59.

6: REELECTION AND ITS UNHAPPY AFTERMATH

88 New Year's Day in 2003 . . . "strong wartime leader": Rove, *Courage and Consequence*, pp. 361–63.
88 he would be willing to step aside: Cheney, *In My Time*, pp. 417–18; Bush, *Decision Points*, pp. 86–87.
89 Bush hoped to run against Howard Dean . . . a more formidable opponent: Bush, *Decision Points*, p. 287.
90 he reversed course and decided to endorse the measure: Elizabeth Bumiller, "Bush Signs Bill Aimed at Fraud in Corporations," *New York Times*, July 31, 2002.
90 "$28,000 for ulcer surgery": Bush, *Decision Points*, p. 281.
91 "through private insurance plans": Ibid., p. 282.
92 largest single-nation health initiative . . . 4.5 million people: Tiaji Salaam-Blyther, "The President's Emergency Plan for AIDS Relief," Congressional Research Service, Congressional Research Report 7-5700, September 27, 2013.
93 "Stuff happens": Donald Rumsfeld news conference, April 11, 2003.
93 "My answer is: Bring 'em on": George W. Bush at White House news conference, July 2, 2003.
93 "trumped their aversion to empire": Bush, *Decision Points*, p. 268.
94 "We never recovered fully": Rice, *No Higher Honor*, p. 274.
94 "I considered it a low point" . . . He also felt blindsided: Bush, *Decision Points*, pp. 88–89.
95 The most dramatic of the battles: This section is based on the definitive, detailed account in Gellman, *Angler*, pp. 277–326.
96 "I never wanted to be blindsided like that again": Bush, *Decision Points*, p. 174.
96 "There's our our opening": Ibid., p. 288.
97 "I had no role in any of it": Rove, *Courage and Consequence*, p. 390.
98 "a buoyant confidence reminiscent of Truman and F.D.R.": William Safire, "Bush's Freedom Speech," *New York Times*, January 21, 2005.
99 these political dynamics were reversed: David S. Broder, "Social Security's Capitol Divide," *Washington Post*, February 20, 2005.
100 had argued that Brown lacked the qualifications: Rove, *Courage and Consequence*, p. 449.
101 "Brownie, you're doing a heck of a job!": George W. Bush remarks at Mobile Regional Airport, September 2, 2005.
101 "I took too long to decide": Bush, *Decision Points*, p. 310.
102 "deeply anchored": Linda Greenhouse, "A Judge Anchored in Modern Law," *New York Times*, July 20, 2005.
102 "The issue is their nonexistence": Charles Krauthammer, "Withdraw This Nominee," *Washington Post*, October 7, 2005.
104 "much of my political capital was gone": Bush, *Decision Points*, p. 330.

104   "black sites": Dana Priest, "CIA Holds Terror Suspects in Secret
      Prisons," *Washington Post*, November 2, 2005.
104   the *New York Times* revealed the existence: James Risen and Eric
      Lichtblau, "Bush Lets U.S. Spy on Callers Without Courts," *New
      York Times*, December 16, 2005.
105   resulted in errors: Rice, *No Higher Honor*, p. 106.
105   more than three thousand Iraqi civilians were killed: http://icasual
      ties.org.
105   "It's failing": Rice, *No Higher Honor*, p. 515.
105   retired generals publicly called for the ouster of Rumsfeld: David S.
      Cloud and Eric Schmitt, "More Retired Generals Call for Rumsfeld's
      Resignation," *New York Times*, April 14, 2006.
106   "I'm the decider": White House news conference, April 18, 2006.
106   Mitch McConnell . . . told Bush: Bush, *Decision Points*, p. 355.
106   The election had little to do with Iraq: Rove, *Courage and Conse-
      quence*, pp. 460–70.
106   "It was a thumping": George W. Bush, White House news confer-
      ence, November 8, 2006.

7. SECOND-TERM CHANGES

108   "He turned and was out the door fast": Cheney, *In My Time*, pp.
      442–43.
108   "Cheney?": Gates, *Duty*, p. 7.
109   without Rumsfeld's input . . . "I could barely contain my joy": Rice,
      No Higher Honor, pp. 540–41.
109   "on the same page": Gates, *Duty*, p. 99.
109   Syria was secretly building a nuclear reactor: This account is based
      on the memoirs of Bush, Cheney, and Rice: Bush, *Decision Points*,
      pp. 420–22; Cheney, *In My Time*, pp. 465–73; Rice, *No Higher
      Honor*, p. 708.
109   "Tojo option": Gates, *Duty*, p. 174.
110   Bush called in his advisers: Bush, *Decision Points*, pp. 413–14; Rice,
      No Higher Honor, pp. 490–91.
110   the Bush administration would be willing to talk: Glenn Kessler,
      "U.S. Will Join Talks with Iran and Syria," *Washington Post*, February
      28, 2007.
111   "Hill and Rice made concession after concession": Cheney, *In My
      Time*, p. 474.
111   negotiations collapsed: Steven Lee Myers, "Nuclear Negotiations
      with North Korea Collapse," *New York Times*, December 12,
      2008.
112   as a bargaining chip: James Mann, *The Obamians: The Struggle
      Inside the White House to Redefine American Power* (New York:
      Viking Press, 2012), p. 197.

112   "no more U-turns to pull": Leonard Doyle, "Condi's Coup: How the
       Neo-Cons Lost the Argument over Iran," *Independent*, July 18, 2008.
112   a new unit, the Office of Terrorism and Financial Intelligence:
       Mann, *Obamians*, pp. 194–96.
113   Although Cheney had proposed military action: Gates, *Duty*, p. 191.
113   "ending tyranny in our world": John Lewis Gaddis, "Ending Tyranny:
       The Past and Future of an Idea," *The American Interest*, September/
       October 2008, vol. 4 (1), pp. 6–15.
114   the "Arab spring" of 2005: Charles Krauthammer, "Syria and the
       New Axis of Evil," *Washington Post*, April 1, 2005.
114   "A democratic Egypt" . . . one-on-one session with the Egyptian
       leader . . . "more rapid change": Rice, *No Higher Honor*, pp. 324–27.
114   "only when we liked the projected outcome": Bush, *Decision Points*,
       p. 406.
115   Bush, however, ordered the speech rewritten: Peter Baker, *Days of
       Fire: Bush and Cheney in the White House* (New York: Doubleday,
       2013), p. 591.
116   "I wanted the people inside Burma": Laura Bush, *Spoken from the
       Heart*, p. 394.
116   "the toughest and most unpopular decision": Bush, *Decision Points*,
       p. 355.
117   take its hand off the bicycle seat: See, for example, "If you're not
       willing to take your hand off the bicycle seat, the person will never
       learn to ride": Rumsfeld, *Known and Unknown*, p. 667.
117   Petraeus spoke almost daily with Meghan O'Sullivan: Fred Kaplan,
       *The Insurgents: David Petraeus and the Plot to Change the American
       Way of War* (New York: Simon & Schuster, 2013), p. 198.
118   "unloaded on him": Gates, *Duty*, p. 39.
118   "I do not believe that more American troops": Thomas E. Ricks,
       *The Gamble: General Petraeus and the American Military Adventure
       in Iraq* (New York: Penguin Press, 2009), p. 92.
118   "So what's your plan, Condi?": Rice, *No Higher Honor*, p. 544.
118   "grave and deteriorating": James A. Baker III and Lee H. Hamilton
       (cochairs), *The Iraq Study Group Report* (New York: Vintage Books,
       2006), p. xiii.
119   "a short-term redeployment or surge": Kaplan, *Insurgents*, pp. 205–7.
119   "we need to change our strategy in Iraq . . . The situation in Iraq is
       unacceptable": George W. Bush, "Address to the Nation on Iraq,"
       January 10, 2007.
119   only 35 percent of Americans: Gallup Poll, http://www.gallup.com
       /poll/116500/presidential-approval-ratings-george-bush.aspx.
120   Senate Republican leaders seemed to be wavering: David E. Sanger,
       "In White House, Debate Is Rising on Iraq Pullback," *New York
       Times*, July 9, 2007.
120   "I want everyone to stay home": Rice, *No Higher Honor*, pp. 589–90.

120   combat forces could be cut back: Ricks, *Gamble*, p. 248.

121   "really require the willing suspension of disbelief": Michael Abramowitz and Jonathan Weisman, "Bush to Endorse Petraeus Plan; Democrats, Some Republicans Seek a Faster Withdrawal," *Washington Post*, September 12, 2007.

121   112 American fatalities . . . 126 . . . just 13: http://icasualties.org /Iraq/ByMonth.aspx.

121   he persuaded himself that a deadline was acceptable: Bush, *Decision Points*, p. 390.

122   The Obama forces portrayed McCain as more conservative than Bush: Mann, *The Obamians*, p. 98.

123   "it's a size-ten shoe that he threw": Sudarsan Raghavan and Dan Eggen, "Bush Ducks Shoe Thrown in Iraq, Continues to Afghanistan," *Washington Post*, December 15, 2008.

8: "I'M GOING TO BE ROOSEVELT, NOT HOOVER"

124   breakfast of cereal and fruit . . . lunch of carrots, a chopped apple, and a hot dog: Gates, *Duty*, p. 57; Henry M. Paulson Jr., *On the Brink: Inside the Race to Stop the Collapse of the Global Financial System* (New York: Business Plus, 2010), p. 424.

124   Republican National Convention: Baker, *Days of Fire*, p. 606.

124   "an otherwise calm fall": Laura Bush, *Spoken from the Heart*, p. 419.

125   "I'm going to be Roosevelt, not Hoover": Bush, *Decision Points*, p. 440.

126   "heart of the country disdain . . . genuine contempt": Paulson, *On the Brink*, pp. 5, 256.

126   won a series of assurances: Andrew Ross Sorkin, *Too Big to Fail: The Inside Story of How Wall Street and Washington Fought to Save the Financial System—and Themselves* (New York: Viking, 2009), pp. 41–43.

126   "little chance to make a mark": Paul Blustein, "Treasury Nominee Has Ties to China," *Washington Post*, June 6, 2006.

127   "most unlikely . . . simmer down": Edmund L. Andrews, "Greenspan Says Housing Boom Is Nearly Over," *New York Times*, August 28, 2005; Paul Krugman, "Greenspan and the Bubble," *New York Times*, August 29, 2005.

128   "an enormous amount of leverage—and risk": Paulson, *On the Brink*, pp. 45–47.

128   "largely contained": Ibid., p. 66; Alan Blinder, *After the Music Stopped: The Financial Crisis, the Response, and the Work Ahead* (New York: Penguin, 2013), p. 88.

128   a short, V-shaped recession: Paulson, *On the Brink*, p. 86.

129   "We're not going to do a bailout, are we?": Ibid., p. 92.

129   "I'm coming to you as an optimistic fellow": Text of George W. Bush speech to the Economic Club of New York, March 14, 2008.

129 "You'll have to explain why it was necessary": Paulson, *On the Brink*, p. 113.

129 "how much it was willing to kick in": David Wessel, *In Fed We Trust: Ben Bernanke's War on the Great Panic* (New York: Crown Business, 2009), p. 147.

130 seventeen proposals for reform: Bush, *Decision Points*, p. 455.

130 "save their ass": Paulson, *On the Brink*, p. 144.

130 foreign governments were weighing in: See Wessel, *In Fed We Trust*, p. 182.

131 "We'll Protect Taxpayers": John McCain and Sarah Palin, "We'll Protect Taxpayers from More Bailouts," *Wall Street Journal*, September 9, 2008.

131 "fed up with bailouts": Paulson, *On the Brink*, p. 180.

131 "I'm being called Mr. Bailout": Wessel, *In Fed We Trust*, p. 14.

131 "What the hell is going on?": Bush, *Decision Points*, p. 456.

131 was not going to keep bailing out failing companies: Sorkin, *Too Big to Fail*, p. 374.

132 "all hell broke loose": Bush, *Decision Points*, p. 457.

132 "If you are comfortable": Wessel, *In Fed We Trust*, p. 196.

133 He questioned Paulson closely: Paulson, *On the Brink*, p. 235.

133 "that was a hell of a lot better than a financial collapse": Bush, *Decision Points*, p. 458.

133 Bush, too, sought to discourage the word: Ibid., p. 454.

134 "Is that enough?" . . . single biggest expenditure: Sorkin, *Too Big to Fail*, pp. 440, 466.

134 a single Republican in the delegation from Texas: Cheney, *In My Time*, p. 509.

135 he found Obama to be thoughtful and supportive, while McCain worried him: Paulson, *On the Brink*, pp. 226, 278.

135 "this sucker could go down": Sorkin, *Too Big to Fail*, p. 489.

135 "very much at ease . . . added nothing of substance": Cheney, *In My Time*, p. 509.

136 "Well, I've clearly lost control": Paulson, *On the Brink*, p. 299.

136 "Are you asking me or telling me?": Ibid., p. 393.

137 "Just don't let Citi fail": Ibid., p. 404.

137 "I had to safeguard American workers": Bush, *Decision Points*, p. 469.

138 "Just make up your mind": Ibid., p. 105.

138 "leaving a good man wounded on the field of battle": Cheney, *In My Time*, p. 410.

EPILOGUE

139 "To know the man is to like the man": CNN Transcript, George W. Bush Presidential Library Opening, April 25, 2013.

140 "No president of my party": Ibid.

140 world's largest purchaser of condoms: Bush, *Decision Points*, 349.

140 he canceled . . . a speech in Geneva: Ewen MacAskill and Afua Hirsch, "George Bush Calls Off Visit to Switzerland," *Guardian*, February 6, 2011.

140 "replenish the ol' coffers": Robert Draper, *Dead Certain: The Presidency of George W. Bush* (New York: Free Press, 2007), p. 406.

140 140 paid talks: Center for Public Integrity, http://www.publicinteg rity.org/2011/05/20/4685/after-skipping-ground-zero-event -obama-bush-made-three-paid-speeches.

141 "I think it's bad for the country": James O'Toole, "George W. Bush Avoids Controversy in Visit to Pittsburgh," *Pittsburgh Post–Gazette*, November 15, 2013.

142 "OMG! Pigs fly. I like something about George W. Bush": Jerry Saltz, "George W. Bush Is a Good Painter," "Vulture" website of *New York* magazine, http://www.vulture.com/2013/02/jerry-saltz -george-w-bush-is-a-good-painter.html.

142 "he was desperate for a pastime": Mark K. Updegrove, "President George W. and Laura Bush Reflect on the Twins, Bush's Newfound Passion for Painting, and More," *Parade*, April 19, 2013, full website transcript, http://parade.condenast.com/5964/markupdegrove/pres ident-george-w-and-laura-bush-reflect-on-the-twins-bushs-new found-passion-for-painting-and-more/.

142 "Painting has changed my life": Rick Klein, "George W. Bush: Painting Has Changed My Life," ABC News "The Note" blog, April 24, 2014, http://abcnews.go.com/blogs/politics/2013/04/george-w-bush -painting-has-changed-my-life.

142 "Six years from now": Draper, *Dead Certain*, p. 407.

143 Harry Truman's presidency and Gerald Ford's pardon: Bush, *Decision Points*, pp. 476–77.

146 "Somebody has got to be risk-averse": Gates, *Duty*, p. 73.

Milestones

1946   Born on July 6 in New Haven, Connecticut.

1948   Father, George H. W. Bush, moves his family to West Texas.

1953   Younger sister Robin dies of leukemia at age four.

1959   The Bush family moves from Midland to Houston, where George W. attends Kinkaid School.

1961   Enters Phillips Academy in Andover, Massachusetts.

1964   Graduates from Andover and enters Yale College. His father runs for the U.S. Senate, but is defeated.

1966   His father wins a seat in Congress.

1968   Graduates from Yale and enters the Texas National Guard.

1970   Finishes active duty in Texas National Guard. Works in his father's unsuccessful Senate campaign against Lloyd Bentsen.

1972   Moves to Alabama to work on unsuccessful Senate campaign of Winton Blount.

1973   Enters Harvard Business School.

1975   Graduates from business school, visits his parents in China, moves back to Midland to start a career in the oil business.

1976   Arrested in Kennebunkport for driving under the influence of alcohol.

1977   Creates his first oil company, Arbusto. Declares his candidacy for Congress. Marries Laura Welch in Midland.

1978   Loses the race for Congress after his opponent portrays him as a "liberal Northeast Republican."

1980   His father is elected vice president.

1981   Becomes the father of twins, Barbara and Jenna.

1986   Turns forty, decides to give up drinking, becomes an evangeli-
       cal Christian. Arranges the sale of his company to Harken
       Energy, ending a decade of involvement in the oil business.

1987   Moves to Washington to help run his father's presidential cam-
       paign.

1988   His father is elected the forty-first president of the United States.

1989   Moves from Washington to Dallas. Leads an ownership group
       that purchases the Texas Rangers baseball team.

1992   His father is defeated for reelection, bringing his political career
       to an end.

1994   Elected governor of Texas.

1998   On a weekend in Kennebunkport, his father introduces him to
       Condoleezza Rice, who begins to put together a group of foreign-
       policy advisers. He wins reelection in Texas and emerges as an
       early front-runner for the Republican presidential nomination.
       His brother Jeb is elected governor of Florida.

1999   Formally declares his candidacy for president. Several other can-
       didates, including Jack Kemp, Elizabeth Dole, and Dan Quayle,
       drop out for lack of funds, leaving John McCain as his main
       rival.

2000   Wins Iowa caucuses but loses New Hampshire primary to
       McCain. Defeats McCain in South Carolina primary and wins
       the nomination.

       Selects Dick Cheney as his running mate.

       November election is disputed and delayed for a month when
       Democratic nominee Al Gore challenges results from Florida.
       In the case of *Bush v. Gore*, Supreme Court votes five to four
       to reject Gore's appeal, awarding Florida and therefore the elec-
       tion to Bush.

2001   Sworn in as the forty-third president of the United States.

       Wins passage from Congress of first set of tax cuts, reducing
       taxes on income.

       Rejects Kyoto Protocol on climate change.

       Bans stem-cell research except for that from existing cell lines.

       September 11 attacks on World Trade Center and Pentagon.

       American and allied forces attack Afghanistan and force Tali-
       ban regime from power but fail to capture Osama bin Laden
       as he flees the country.

Authorizes National Security Agency to conduct new Terrorist Surveillance Program.

Notifies Russia that the United States will withdraw from the Anti-Ballistic Missile Treaty.

Asks Tommy Franks, commander of U.S. forces in the Middle East, to develop first war plan for attacking Iraq.

2002   Signs No Child Left Behind legislation.

Says in State of the Union address that Iraq, Iran, and North Korea form an "axis of evil."

First prisoners arrive at new U.S. facility in Guantánamo Bay, Cuba.

Authorizes CIA to use harsh interrogation techniques, including waterboarding, for detainees held at "black sites" overseas.

Signs Sarbanes-Oxley legislation establishing new requirements for corporate boards, management, and accounting firms.

Announces in speech at West Point that United States will take "preemptive action" to safeguard national security.

Wins passage from Congress of Authorization for the Use of Military Force against Iraq.

Republicans gain seats in midterm elections.

U.N. Security Council approves resolution giving Saddam Hussein a "final opportunity" to disclose his nuclear weapons program and to give it up.

2003   In State of Union speech, announces plans for PEPFAR, the President's Emergency Plan for AIDS Relief.

Colin Powell appears before U.N. Security Council to outline U.S. evidence that Iraq possesses weapons of mass destruction.

Tries but fails to obtain new U.N. Security Council resolution authorizing military action against Iraq.

United States and coalition forces invade Iraq, capture Baghdad; Saddam Hussein flees; Bush announces end of major combat operations before a banner that reads MISSION ACCOMPLISHED.

Wins approval of second set of tax cuts, reducing rates on dividends and capital gains.

Amid widening chaos in Iraq, United Nations representative Sergio Vieira de Mello is killed in the bombing of the U.N.'s Baghdad headquarters.

Congress approves Bush's proposal for prescription drug benefit under Medicare.

Libyan leader Muammar Gadhafi agrees to give up nuclear weapons program.

U.S. forces capture Saddam Hussein.

2004 Photos of American soldiers abusing prisoners at Abu Ghraib prison become public.

Defeats John Kerry to win a second term as president.

Announces that Colin Powell will step down and Condoleezza Rice will replace him as secretary of state.

2005 In second inaugural address, says United States has "the ultimate goal of ending tyranny in our world."

Proposes far-reaching changes in Social Security to move toward private accounts. Congress declines to act on his proposal.

Iraq holds elections, with large turnout.

Hurricane Katrina strikes Gulf Coast and New Orleans; Bush is slow to respond.

Nominates John Roberts to Supreme Court to replace Sandra Day O'Connor, then nominates Roberts as chief justice of the United States after the death of William Rehnquist. Nominates Harriet Miers as associate justice, but she withdraws her name; nominates Samuel Alito. Roberts and Alito are confirmed.

I. Lewis Libby, Cheney's chief of staff, is indicted for perjury.

2006 Iraq deteriorates into sectarian strife after bombing of the Golden Mosque in Samarra.

Appoints Ben Bernanke to be chairman of Federal Reserve Board.

Supreme Court rules in *Hamdan v. Rumsfeld* that some parts of Bush's war on terror are illegal or unconstitutional. In response, CIA closes "black sites" and halts some of its harsh interrogation techniques.

Appoints Henry Paulson as new secretary of the treasury.

North Korea conducts first nuclear test.

In midterm elections, Democrats take control of both House and Senate.

Fires Rumsfeld and appoints Robert Gates to take his place as secretary of defense.

Signs agreement for civilian nuclear cooperation with India, opening the way for new strategic relationship between the two countries.

Saddam Hussein is executed.

2007   Orders surge in American forces to Iraq; appoints David Petraeus to take command and to carry out new strategy of counterinsurgency.

Convenes Annapolis conference on the Middle East.

2008   Treasury Department arranges rescue of Bear Stearns.

U.S. government establishes conservatorship over Fannie Mae and Freddie Mac.

Lehman Brothers files for bankruptcy; financial system freezes up; stock market plunges.

Treasury Department arranges rescue of AIG.

Congress enacts $700 billion Troubled Asset Relief Program (TARP).

Barack Obama is elected America's forty-fourth president, defeating John McCain.

Convenes first-ever G-20 summit meeting.

Provides funds for short-term bailout of auto industry.

Signs agreement with Iraq on departure of U.S. forces from the country by the end of 2011.

2009   Rejects appeals from Cheney to pardon Libby.

Leaves office and returns to Texas.

2010   Memoir *Decision Points* is published.

2013   Hacked email accounts show Bush has taken up painting.

Opening of George W. Bush Presidential Library and Museum in Dallas.

Selected Bibliography

BOOKS

Baker, Peter. *Days of Fire: Bush and Cheney in the White House*. New York: Doubleday, 2013.

Blinder, Alan. *After the Music Stopped: The Financial Crisis, the Response, and the Work Ahead*. New York: Penguin, 2013.

Bruni, Frank. *Ambling into History: The Unlikely Odyssey of George W. Bush*. New York: HarperCollins, 2002.

Bush, Barbara. *Barbara Bush: A Memoir*. New York: Charles Scribner's Sons, 1994.

Bush, George W. *A Charge to Keep*. New York: Harper Perennial, 2001.

———. *Decision Points*. New York: Crown, 2010.

Bush, Laura. *Spoken from the Heart*. New York: Charles Scribner's Sons, 2010.

Cannon, Carl M., Lou Dubose, and Jan Reid. *Boy Genius*. New York: PublicAffairs, 2003.

Cheney, Dick. *In My Time: A Personal and Political Memoir*. New York: Threshold Editions, 2011.

Clarke, Richard A. *Against All Enemies: Inside America's War on Terror*. New York: Free Press, 2004.

Cramer, Richard Ben. *What It Takes: The Way to the White House*. New York: Random House, 1992.

DeYoung, Karen. *Soldier: The Life of Colin Powell*. New York: Alfred A. Knopf, 2006.

Draper, Robert. *Dead Certain: The Presidency of George W. Bush*. New York: Free Press, 2007.

Engel, Jeffrey A., ed. *The China Diary of George H. W. Bush: The Making of a Global President*. Princeton: Princeton University Press, 2008.

Feith, Douglas J. *War and Decision: Inside the Pentagon at the Dawn of the War on Terrorism*. New York: HarperCollins, 2008.

Frank, Justin A. *Bush on the Couch: Inside the Mind of the President*. New York: ReganBooks, 2004.

Gates, Robert M. *Duty: Memoirs of a Secretary at War*. New York: Alfred A. Knopf, 2014.

Gellman, Barton. *Angler: The Cheney Vice Presidency*. New York: Penguin, 2008.

Ivins, Molly, and Lou Dubose. *Bushwhacked: Life in George W. Bush's America*. New York: Random House, 2003.

Kaplan, Fred. *The Insurgents: David Petraeus and the Plot to Change the American Way of War*. New York: Simon & Schuster, 2013.

Kennedy, Edward M. *True Compass*. New York: Twelve, 2009.

Mann, James. *The Obamians: The Struggle Inside the White House to Redefine American Power*. New York: Viking, 2012.

———. *Rise of the Vulcans: The History of Bush's War Cabinet*. New York: Viking, 2004.

Mayer, Jane. *The Dark Side: The Inside Story of How the War on Terror Turned into a War on American Ideals*. New York: Doubleday, 2008.

National Commission on Terrorist Attacks. *The 9/11 Commission Report*. New York: W. W. Norton, 2004.

Paulson, Henry M., Jr. *On the Brink: Inside the Race to Stop the Collapse of the Global Financial System*. New York: Business Plus, 2010.

Powell, Colin. *My American Journey*. New York: Ballantine, 1995.

Rice, Condoleezza. *No Higher Honor: A Memoir of My Years in Washington*. New York: Crown, 2011.

Rove, Karl. *Courage and Consequence: My Life as a Conservative in the Fight*. New York: Threshold Editions, 2010.

Rumsfeld, Donald. *Known and Unknown*. New York: Sentinel, 2011.

Sorkin, Andrew Ross. *Too Big to Fail: The Inside Story of How Wall Street and Washington Fought to Save the Financial System—and Themselves*. New York: Viking, 2009.

Suskind, Ron. *The Price of Loyalty: George W. Bush, the White House, and the Education of Paul O'Neill*. New York: Simon & Schuster, 2004.

Tenet, George. *At the Center of the Storm: My Years at the CIA*. New York: HarperCollins, 2007.

Toobin, Jeffrey. *Too Close to Call: The Thirty-Six-Day Battle to Decide the 2000 Election*. New York: Random House, 2001.

Weisberg, Jacob. *The Bush Tragedy*. New York: Random House, 2008.

Wessel, David. *In Fed We Trust: Ben Bernanke's War on the Great Panic*. New York: Crown Business, 2009.

Zeldin, Charles L. *Bush v. Gore: Exposing the Hidden Crisis in American Democracy*. Lawrence: University of Kansas Press, 2010.

ARTICLES

Specific magazine and newspaper articles are listed in the footnotes. But I found the following articles and newspaper series of particular help in tracing the life and career of George W. Bush before he reached the White House.

Patricia Kilday Hart, "Don't Call Him Junior," *Texas Monthly*, August 1988.

David Maraniss, "The Bush Bunch," *Washington Post Magazine*, January 22, 1989.

Patrick Beach, "The First Son: George W. Bush Had His Rebellions," *Austin American–Statesman*, June 13, 1999.

The *Washington Post* series by Lois Romano and George Lardner Jr. entitled "The Life of George W. Bush," which appeared from July 25 to July 31, 1999:

Lois Romano and George Lardner Jr., "1986: A Life-Changing Year; Epiphany Fueled Candidate's Climb," *Washington Post*, July 25, 1999.

George Lardner Jr. and Lois Romano, "A Texas Childhood; A Sister Dies, a Family Moves On; Loss Creates Strong Bond Between Mother, Son," *Washington Post*, July 26, 1999.

Lois Romano and George Lardner Jr., "Following His Father's Path—Step by Step by Step," *Washington Post*, July 27, 1999.

George Lardner Jr. and Lois Romano, "At Height of Vietnam, Graduate Picks Guard; With Deferment Over, Pilot Training Begins," *Washington Post*, July 28, 1999.

Lois Romano and George Lardner Jr., "A Run for the House; Courting a Wife, Then the Voters," *Washington Post*, July 29, 1999.

George Lardner Jr. and Lois Romano, "The Turning Point; After Coming Up Dry, Financial Rescues," *Washington Post*, July 30, 1999.

Lois Romano and George Lardner Jr., "Moving Up to the Major Leagues; Father's Campaign, Baseball Provide Foundation for Own Run," *Washington Post*, July 31, 1999.

The *New York Times* series by Nicholas D. Kristof that appeared intermittently from May through October 2000:

Nicholas D. Kristof, "A Philosophy with Roots in Conservative Texas Soil: Governor Bush's Journey: A Boy from Midland," *New York Times*, May 21, 2000.

——, "Earning A's in People Skills at Andover: Governor Bush's Journey: The Cheerleader," *New York Times*, June 10, 2000.

——, "Ally of an Older Generation Amid the Tumult of the 60's: Governor Bush's Journey: Confronting the Counterculture," *New York Times*, June 19, 2000.

——, "Learning How to Run: A West Texas Stumble: Governor Bush's Journey: The First Campaign," *New York Times*, July 27, 2000.

——, "How Bush Came to Tame His Inner Scamp: Governor Bush's Journey: Midlife Redemption," *New York Times*, July 29, 2000.

——, "For Bush, Thrill Was in Father's Chase: Governor Bush's Journey: The 1988 Campaign," *New York Times*, August 29, 2000.

——, "A Father's Footsteps Echo Throughout a Son's Career: Governor Bush's Journey: The Legacy," *New York Times*, September 21, 2000.

——, "Road to Politics Ran Through a Texas Ballpark: Governor Bush's Journey: Breaking into Baseball," *New York Times*, September 24, 2000.

——, "A Master of Bipartisanship with No Taste for Details: Governor Bush's Journey: Running Texas," *New York Times*, October 16, 2000.

——, "For Bush, His Toughest Call Was the Choice to Run at All: Governor Bush's Journey: The Decision," *New York Times*, October 29, 2000.

Acknowledgments

When Sean Wilentz, the general editor of the American Presidents series, first asked me to write this book, I hesitated. I had already covered some of the ground, writing about George W. Bush's foreign-policy team in my earlier book *Rise of the Vulcans* and wasn't sure I wanted to return to a similar subject. Once I agreed to do the book, I saw how wrong I was; this project offered a wonderful chance to trace through a wealth of material about the Bush administration's policies, both foreign and domestic, as well as the upbringing and career of Bush himself. So the first note of thanks goes to Sean for giving me the opportunity to do the book and for providing extremely helpful comments and reactions as the book was being written.

I am also especially grateful to Paul Golob, executive editor at Henry Holt and Company, who took the hands-on role in shepherding this book to completion. I had known Paul casually over the years, in part through the favorable comments of fellow journalist-authors, but had no idea how great an editor he is until he went to work on my own book. He is among the few editors who understand the internal structure and flow of a manuscript. His line editing and attention to detail are, as far as I know, unmatched in the publishing industry.

The next person to whom I am indebted is Christopher Appel. As a graduate student at the Johns Hopkins School of Advanced International Studies, he served as research assistant for much of the period in which this book was written. He helped me to think through in advance what the book needed to cover and to find the materials I needed. After he had graduated and started a new job, he contacted me again and volunteered to read and react to chapters. I had never been willing to let a researcher do this before, but Christopher was so talented that I knew it would be helpful. I was right; it turns out he's a good editor, too.

In addition, another SAIS student, Despoina Sideri, was of great value in the final month of the book, when I was nailing down the final details. These students underscore my good fortune in having been able to write this book at Johns Hopkins SAIS; it is now the fourth book I have written and published while at the school over the past decade. At SAIS, I am indebted to Dean Vali Nasr and former dean Jessica Einhorn, to Carla Freeman and Christine Kunkel in the Foreign Policy Institute, and to Erik Jones, Kathryn Knowles, and Lindsey Ohmit in the European and Eurasian Studies program for supporting me in my work.

As always, my wife, Caroline Dexter, is the bedrock of support for my life. My daughter, Elizabeth, and her husband, Micah Lasher; my son, Ted, and his wife, Kristin; and my grandchildren, Nate, Ben, and Ryan, all keep me in good cheer. Writing books is what I do in between our visits to them.

Index

ABOUT THE AUTHOR

JAMES MANN is the author of six books on American politics and national security issues, including *Rise of the Vulcans: The History of Bush's War Cabinet* and *The Obamians: The Struggle Inside the White House to Redefine American Power.* A longtime correspondent for the *Los Angeles Times*, he is currently a fellow in residence at the Johns Hopkins University School of Advanced International Studies. He lives in Washington, D.C.